MW01174031

SARAH'S GRANDDAUGHTER

25

POUND CAKE

recipes

LAKEISHA DIXON JONES

RED VELVET
VANILLA
OLD FASHION
OREO
PECAN BOURBON
COCONUT
RED VELVET
VANILLA

CHOCOLATE CHIP

WALNUT

OATMEAL RAISIN

PECAN

CHOCOLATE CHIP

WALNUT

CHOCOLATE CHIP

PECAN

thank you

To my beloved grandmothers, who left me with treasures far more precious than silver or gold.

Granny Sarah Smith, my father's mother, you will forever live in my heart. I remember the sweet mornings filled with the scent of sizzling bacon and homemade biscuits, gospel music echoing through the house as you called us all to rise and prepare for church. You packed me and five other grandkids into your car every Sunday, ensuring we understood the value of being in the Lord's house. One Sunday, as I laughed and played in church, you pinched me and said, "Stop playing in the Lord's house. One day, you won't play in church." And now, at the age of 45, I know exactly what you meant. I'm no longer playing—I know Him for myself. You were right, Granny. Your words have come to pass, and I'm no longer bound by dogma but strengthened through relationships.

Both of my grandmothers were gifted in the kitchen—my father's mom was known for her three-layer cakes, pound cakes, biscuits, and pies, while my mother's mom baked sheet cakes, pound cakes, and pies to perfection. While neither of them left me land, riches, or even written recipes, they gave me something even greater. They left me with memories of love, faith, and resilience—memories that have become the foundation of my legacy, my lifestyle, and my enduring pursuit of longevity through sweet love. So, I honor them and their legacy always.

thank you
JUANITA BENTON

A special shout-out to Juanita Benton, who gifted me my very first Sour Cream recipe. Thank you, Juanita, for being a source of inspiration and love for our family with your delicious food, cakes, and cobblers. You have always made the holidays so much more special, filling our hearts and stomachs with your good food and kindness. You are truly an icon, and your love and presence will always be remembered.

With each pound cake I bake, I honor you all—the women who shaped my life and legacy through your hands and hearts. This book is a tribute to the love you poured into your kitchens and into me.

With love and gratitude,
Lakeisha Dixon Jones
Founder of Savory & Sweet Treats

Sarah's Granddaughter: 25 Pound Cake Recipes
Copyright ©2024 by Lakeisha Dixon Jones

For more information, contact Lakeisha Dixon Jones at www.savoryandsweettreatsatl.com or www.lakeishadixonjones.com.

ISBN: 979-8-9901609-5-8 (Hardcover)
ISBN: 979-8-9901609-7-2 (Paperback)

Cover by: Sharon Lewis-Ruff, The Planner Consulting
Editing by: Lakeisha Dixon Jones
Formatting by: Wisdom by 30 Literary Group

Professional Photo Credits
- Rob Ector (Cover Photo)
- Lakeisha Dixon Jones (Desserts)

Recipes in this book may include ingredients such as nuts, dairy, wheat, and soy. Please consider any dietary restrictions and consult with an allergist if necessary before preparing.

Thank You

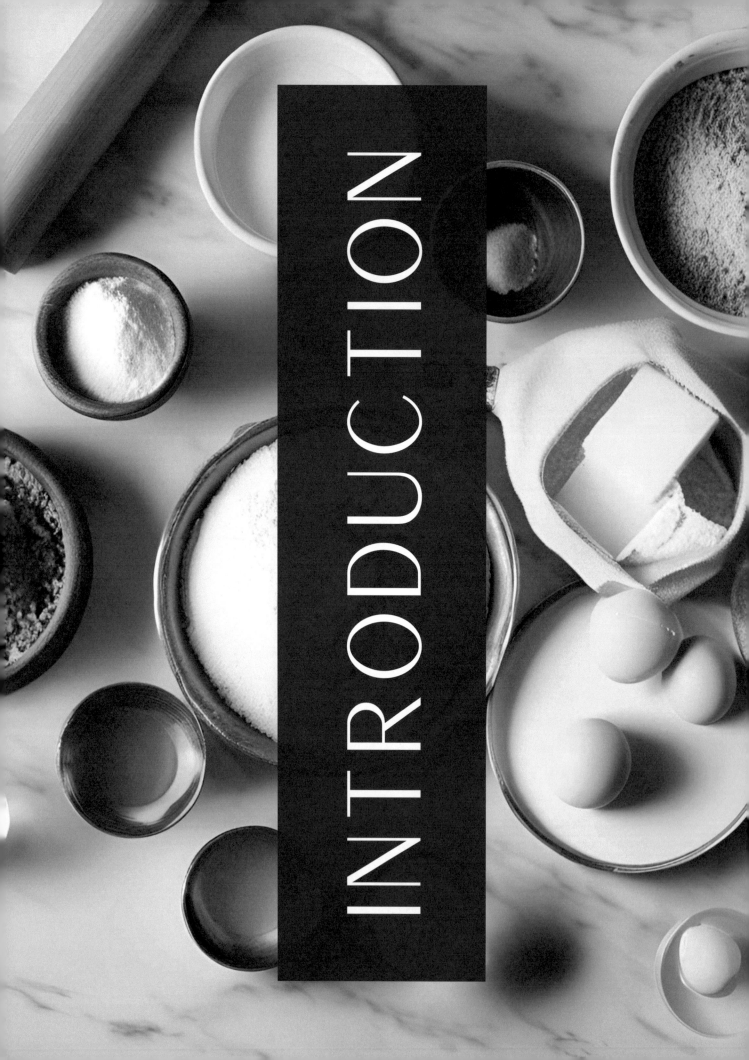

INTRODUCTION

Life has a way of making you pause and reflect on how good God has been. I've always loved people, and more than that, I've loved feeding people. But my true passion lies in baking. I am Lakeisha Dixon Jones, and while many of you may not know me, I've spent nearly 12 years as a Master Certified Life and Professional Coach, guiding people to their breakthrough moments. And for the past five years, I've been running an online bakery, a venture I embraced fully in October of 2022. Little did I know that this journey would become more than just a business—it would be the very thing that healed me and transformed my pain into purpose.

I am a woman who has seen sorrow turned into dancing, and grief transformed into something both purposeful and profitable. Through baking, I found my way back to joy. In less than 2 years, I've had the privilege of coaching over 200 men and women nationwide on how to bake the perfect pound cake. I've studied this timeless dessert and learned its intricacies—not yet mastering it, but gaining a deep understanding of its art. As a third-generation baker, I come from a lineage steeped in faith and food. My grandmothers, Sarah Smith and Estell Dixon, were women of strength, prayer, and resilience.

My Granny Sarah was a spiritual warrior, her days filled with the aroma of homemade biscuits & homemade cakes, the sound of gospel music, and hours spent in prayer at the altar... She took me to prayer services and revivals, leaving me with memories that shaped my soul. My grandmothers didn't leave me land, money, or even recipes, but they left me something far more valuable: the gift of memories, lessons of faith, and a love for baking that became the foundation of my life and business.

On January 1st, 2023, I experienced a devastating loss. I miscarried my first child, and the grief nearly overwhelmed me. I was hurt, angry, and searching for something to help me cope with the pain. It was in the kitchen, with my mixing bowls and pans, that I found the solace I needed. As I measured cups of flour, God measured cups of healing, and slowly, baking became the vessel through which He restored me. In that season, Savory & Sweet Treats began to flourish in ways I could have never imagined. My brand grew rapidly, not just in size but in purpose.

In one year, we baked for millionaires, athletes, doctors, nurses, CEOs, and so many others. We even became Cam Newton's baking coach for a season. It became clear that God was guiding my every step, leading me through a path of baking and business with grace, favor, and flavors. I've learned that when we trust in His timing, our commitment and consistency, mixed with His favor, creates something far sweeter than we ever expected. Now, I welcome you to the world of Savory & Sweet Treats LLC, a business born through trials, testing, and truth. These recipes are more than just cakes—they are love, honor, and a testament to God's faithfulness. Thank you for your support, for believing in the power of my story, and for tasting the legacy I'm building.

...mixed with His favor

CONTENTS

The Legacy of Pound Cake   **11**

The Flours   **14**

The Pan   **17**

The Oven   **21**

The Fridge   **23**

Baker's Kit   **28**

Happy Baking   **33**

Sweet Potato Pound Cake   **34**

Sweet Classic Pound Cake   **36**

Moscato Cream Pound Cake   **40**

Eggnog Pound Cake   **44**

Vanilla Loaf Pound Cake   **48**

Strawberry Swirl Pound Cake   **50**

Sour Cream Pound   **53**

Oreo Sour Cream Pound   **57**

Biscoff Cookie Butter Pound   **60**

Whipping Cream Pound Cake Recipe with Caramel Pecan Sauce   **63**

Red Velvet Pound   **67**

Almond Honey Pound   **71**

Chocolate Buttermilk Pound   **74**

7-Up Cream Pound   **77**

Marble Cream Pound   **80**

Lemon Sour Cream Pound   **84**

Pina Colada Cream Pound   **88**

CONTENTS

7-Flavor Cream Pound Cake   **11**

Coconut Rum Pound Cake   **97**

Lemon Blueberry Pound Cake   **101**

Coconut Lime Pound Cake   **104**

Mountain Dew Pound Cake   **107**

Pecan Bourbon Pound Cake   **110**

Key Lime Pound Cake   **113**

S'mores Pound Cake   **116**

Brown Butter Vanilla Bean Pound Cake   **119**

Birthday Cake Pound   **122**

Orange Grand Marnier Pound Cake   **125**

Peach Cobbler Pound Cake   **128**

Glazes

Orange Cream Glaze & Lemon Cream Glaze   **130**

Vanilla Almond Glaze & 7-Flavor Glaze   **131**

Butter Glaze & Vanilla Butter Glaze   **132**

Chocolate Butter Glaze & Maple Cinnamon Glaze   **133**

Chocolate Espresso Glaze & Coconut Rum Glaze   **134**

Salted Caramel Glaze & Brown Sugar Bourbon Glaze   **135**

Cream Cheese Glaze & Lemon Cream Cheese Glaze   **136**

Maple Cream Cheese Glaze & Cinnamon Cream Cheese Glaze   **137**

Strawberry Cream Cheese Glaze & Chocolate Cream Cheese Glaze   **138**

Bonus Cakes **140**

THE LEGACY

OF POUND CAKE

The origin of the pound cake dates back to the early 18th century in Northern Europe, specifically in Britain. Its name comes from the original recipe, which called for one pound each of four essential ingredients: flour, butter, sugar, and eggs. This simple yet generous formula made the pound cake easy to remember, especially in times when written recipes weren't widely available.

The beauty of the pound cake lay in its straightforwardness. It was a dense, rich cake, born from a time when bakers relied on natural leavening agents like the air beaten into the eggs. The recipe was practical too—large enough to feed a family or community, which was especially valuable in the age of hearth baking.

Over the centuries, the pound cake recipe traveled across Europe and to America, evolving along the way. Variations began to include flavorings such as vanilla, lemon zest, or spices. As baking powder and other chemical leaveners were introduced in the 19th century, the cake became lighter, and different cultures started adding their *own* twists. In the American South, for instance, pound cakes became iconic, with each family adding its signature ingredient—whether it was sour cream, cream cheese, or rich glazes.

Pound cake holds a special place in Southern culture, where it's not just a dessert but a symbol of family gatherings, church socials, and holidays. For many, it represents heritage and legacy, passed down from generation to generation, often without formal recipes. Like in my family, where the exact measurements weren't written, but the love and care poured into each cake spoke louder than words.

In its essence, the pound cake is more than just a cake—it's a story of adaptation, resilience, and community, making it a fitting addition to family traditions across the world. And now, as you hold this recipe book, you are joining that rich legacy, continuing the tradition with your own personal touch.

CLASSIC POUND CAKE

Instructions

1. Preheat your oven to 325°F (163°C). Grease and flour a 10-inch tube pan or bundt pan.

2. Cream the Butter and Sugar: In a large mixing bowl, cream the softened butter and sugar together until the mixture is light and fluffy. This may take about 5-7 minutes.

3. Add the eggs one at a time, beating well after each addition. Scrape down the sides of the bowl as needed.

4. Incorporate Dry Ingredients: In a separate bowl, combine the flour and salt. Gradually add this dry mixture to the butter and sugar mixture, mixing until just combined. Do not overmix.

5. Gently fold in the vanilla extract for added flavor.

6. Bake: Pour the batter into the prepared pan, smoothing the top with a spatula. Bake in the preheated oven for about 1 hour and 15 minutes, or until a toothpick inserted into the center comes out clean.

7. Cool: Allow the cake to cool in the pan for about 10-15 minutes, then carefully invert it onto a wire rack to cool completely.

8. Serve: Once cooled, slice and serve plain or with your favorite glaze or frosting.

Ingredients

- 1 pound (4 sticks) unsalted butter, softened
- 1 pound (2 cups) granulated sugar
- 1 pound (4 large) eggs
- 1 pound (4 cups) all-purpose flour
- 1 teaspoon salt
- 1 teaspoon vanilla extract (optional)

THE FLOURS

EVER WONDERED WHICH FLOURS TO USE FOR PERFECT BAKING?

Let me share my top four favorites and why I love them!

Swans Down Cake Flour

This is my go-to for cakes! Swans Down Cake Flour is made from soft wheat, finely milled to create an incredibly light and delicate texture, which is 27 times finer than regular all-purpose flour. Its low protein content (about 6-8%) ensures cakes turn out soft, tender, and moist, with a smooth crumb and a fine, airy finish. It's perfect for angel food cakes, chiffon cakes, and delicate pastries where a light, fluffy texture is key.

White Lily All-Purpose Flour

A Southern baking classic, White Lily is made from soft winter wheat, which has a lower protein content than most all-purpose flours (around 9%). It's perfect for biscuits, muffins, and cakes because it delivers a lighter, softer crumb and higher rise. Unlike other all-purpose flours, White Lily provides the benefits of a cake flour while still being versatile enough for a range of baked goods like cookies or pancakes. It's a favorite in the South for making tender, flaky biscuits and quick breads.

King Arthur All-Purpose Flour

For consistency and versatility, nothing beats a high-quality all-purpose flour like King Arthur. It has a slightly higher protein content (11-12%), making it perfect for everything from cakes to cookies to bread. It offers a balanced structure and crumb, giving your cakes the right balance of moistness and firmness while supporting a wide range of recipes. It's my go-to for pound cakes, cookies, and even homemade bread!

15

Gold Medal All-Purpose Flour

Gold Medal is a well-loved, dependable all-purpose flour that has been a staple in kitchens for over a century. With a moderate protein content (about 10-11%), it strikes a great balance between strength and tenderness. This makes it ideal for a variety of baked goods, from soft cookies and pie crusts to hearty bread and pizza dough. Its versatility makes it a reliable option whether you're whipping up cakes, quick breads, or pastries, and it produces consistently good results for home bakers of all skill levels.

WHAT ARE LEAVENERS

Leaveners are ingredients that help baked goods rise by creating gas bubbles in the dough or batter. There are three main types of leaveners: chemical, biological, and mechanical. Each works in a different way to create the desired texture in your baked goods.

Chemical Leaveners

These leaveners produce gas through a chemical reaction when mixed with moisture or heat. The gas (usually carbon dioxide) expands in the dough or batter, making it rise.

- Baking Powder: This is a combination of an acid (usually cream of tartar) and a base (baking soda), plus a drying agent like cornstarch. It's double-acting, meaning it releases gas both when it's mixed with liquid and when it's heated, providing a reliable rise in cakes, muffins, and quick breads.

- Baking Soda: This is pure sodium bicarbonate, a base that needs an acidic ingredient (like lemon juice, vinegar, buttermilk, or yogurt) to create carbon dioxide. It's commonly used in recipes with acidic components to help baked goods rise. Baking soda works immediately upon mixing, so baked goods with baking soda should be baked promptly.

Biological Leaveners

These leaveners involve living organisms that produce gas through fermentation. They take longer to act but provide distinct flavors and textures, particularly in bread.

- Yeast: Yeast is a living organism that ferments sugars in the dough, producing carbon dioxide and alcohol. The carbon dioxide creates bubbles in the dough, causing it to rise, while the alcohol adds flavor and evaporates during baking. Yeast-leavened breads like sourdough, challah, and baguettes typically take longer to rise due to the fermentation process.

- Sourdough Starter: A type of yeast leavener made from wild yeast and bacteria (lactobacilli) naturally occurring in flour. It's a fermented mixture of flour and water, and the wild yeast and bacteria work together to leaven the dough. Sourdough imparts a tangy flavor and a chewy texture to bread due to the long fermentation process.

Mechanical Leaveners

These leaveners don't rely on chemicals or organisms but instead trap air or steam within the batter or dough to help it rise.

- Beating and Whisking: Mechanical leavening occurs when you incorporate air into ingredients like butter, eggs, or cream. For example, when you cream butter and sugar together for a cake, the process traps tiny air bubbles in the fat, which expand during baking, creating a lighter texture. Whisking egg whites for meringues or soufflés adds air into the mixture, which helps give them lift and volume as they bake.

- Steam: When moisture in the dough turns to steam in the oven, it expands and lifts the dough. This is the primary leavening agent in recipes like puff pastry, choux pastry (for éclairs and cream puffs), and popovers, where high heat helps create rapid steam production for a light, airy structure.

THE PAN

BEST WAY TO GREASE A POUND CAKE PAN
(BUNDT OR TUBE)

1 Greasing a pound cake pan properly ensures your cake releases easily after baking. Here's the best method to grease a pound cake pan, including options for butter, shortening, and baking spray:

Choose the Right Greasing Method:
- Butter: Use salted butter for a flavorful crust.
- Shortening: Solid shortening provides a reliable non-stick surface.
- Baking Spray: Non-stick baking spray, especially those containing flour, offers a convenient option for easy release. My personal favorite is (Pam's Baking Spray with Flour)

2 **Steps to Grease the Pan:**
Prepare Your Pan:
- Ensure the pound cake pan is clean and dry before greasing.

Apply the Grease:
- If using butter or shortening:
  - Take a piece of parchment paper or a clean paper towel, and apply a generous amount of butter or shortening to it.
  - Spread an even layer of grease over the bottom and sides of the pan, covering all corners and crevices.
- If using baking spray:
  - Hold the spray can about 6 inches away from the pan and spray an even coat over the bottom and sides, ensuring all areas are covered.

Add Flour:
- After greasing the pan (whether with butter or shortening), sprinkle a tablespoon or two of all-purpose flour evenly over the greased surfaces.
- Tap and Shake: Hold the pan at an angle and gently tap it, shaking it to ensure the flour coats the greased surfaces evenly on both the bottom and sides.

3 Remove Excess Flour:

- After coating, tap the pan gently over the sink or trash can to remove any excess flour, preventing flour residue on the cake.

Using any of these methods—or a combination—will help ensure that your pound cake releases perfectly from the pan, showcasing that beautiful, moist cake!

THE OVEN

THE IMPORTANCE OF PRE-HEATING THE OVEN

Preheating the oven is vital for achieving the perfect pound cake. It ensures consistent baking, activates leavening agents for proper rising, develops desirable textures and flavors, allows for accurate cooking times, and promotes food safety. Always preheat your oven according to the recipe instructions for the best results with your pound cake!

1 Consistent Cooking Temperature

- Even Baking: Pound cakes require a steady temperature for even cooking. Preheating ensures that the oven reaches the desired temperature before you place your batter inside, resulting in a cake that bakes uniformly throughout.

- Avoiding Temperature Shock: Placing your pound cake batter in a cold oven can lead to uneven baking. The edges may cook faster than the center, resulting in a cake that is dry around the edges and undercooked in the middle.

2 Proper Rising

- Leavening Agent Activation: Pound cakes typically rely on baking powder or baking soda for leavening. Preheating the oven allows these leavening agents to activate properly, ensuring that your pound cake rises beautifully and has a light, fluffy texture.

- Preventing Dense Cakes: Starting with a preheated oven helps to prevent the cake from becoming dense or heavy. A cold oven can hinder the rise, leading to a denser cake than desired.

3 Texture and Flavor Development

- Maillard Reaction: Preheating is essential for the Maillard reaction, which contributes to the delicious, golden-brown crust of your pound cake. This reaction begins at high temperatures, so starting with a preheated oven is key to achieving that perfect color and flavor.

- Crisp Crust: A preheated oven helps form a crisp outer crust while maintaining a moist interior, a hallmark of a well-baked pound cake.

4 Accurate Cooking Time

- Predictable Results: Recipes for pound cakes are typically designed with preheating in mind. By preheating your oven, you can rely on the recommended baking time in the recipe for consistent results.
- Avoiding Over or Undercooking: If the oven isn't preheated, the baking time can be inaccurate, leading to overbaking or underbaking your pound cake, which can affect its flavor and texture.

5 Food Safety

- Bacterial Growth Prevention: Baking batter that contains perishable ingredients (like eggs and dairy) in a cold oven can allow it to sit at unsafe temperatures for too long, increasing the risk of bacterial growth. Preheating helps ensure that the cake starts baking immediately, keeping it safe to eat.

THE FRIDGE

DON'T FORGET TO TAKE YOUR INGREDIENTS OUT OF THE FRIDGE AND HERE'S WHY

I want you to *really* understand the importance of room-temperature ingredients when baking. It's a game-changer, especially for our beloved pound cakes!

Using ingredients at room temperature helps everything blend together more smoothly, creating that perfect texture we all love. It ensures even mixing, allowing for better flavor development and a light, airy crumb. Remember, baking is not a competition; it's love! So let's take our time and make every cake a delicious labor of love.

1 Better Emulsification

- Creaming Process: When you cream butter and sugar together, having both at room temperature allows them to blend together smoothly. This process helps to incorporate air into the batter, leading to a lighter and fluffier pound cake.
- Uniform Mixture: Cold ingredients can lead to a lumpy or uneven batter, making it difficult for the ingredients to emulsify properly.

2 Improved Texture

- Consistent Baking: Room temperature ingredients mix more uniformly, which contributes to a consistent texture throughout the cake. This is especially crucial for pound cakes, where a dense and uniform crumb is desired.
- Avoiding Dense Cakes: If cold ingredients are added to the batter, they can cause the batter to cool down, preventing it from rising properly during baking and resulting in a denser cake.

3 Enhanced Flavor

- Flavor Development: Ingredients like butter and eggs at room temperature can blend better, allowing their flavors to meld and develop more effectively. This results in a richer-tasting pound cake.

- Better Integration of Add-Ins: Room temperature ingredients ensure that any additional flavors or ingredients, like extracts or spices, are incorporated evenly throughout the batter.

4 More Predictable Results

- Consistent Baking Times: Using room temperature ingredients helps to ensure that your pound cake bakes evenly, leading to more predictable results in terms of texture, rise, and overall quality.
- Reducing Temperature Shock: Cold ingredients can create a temperature shock, which may affect the way the batter rises in the oven, leading to inconsistent baking outcomes.

5 Ease of Mixing

- Simpler Process: Room-temperature ingredients are easier to mix, reducing the effort needed to achieve a smooth batter. This can save time and energy, making the baking process more enjoyable.

HERE'S ANOTHER FREQUENTLY ASKED QUESTION: HOW LONG DOES IT TAKE TO TEMP INGREDIENTS

1 Butter

- Time: About 30 to 60 minutes.
- Tips: Cut it into smaller pieces to speed up the process, or you can grate it if you're in a hurry.

2 Eggs

- Time: About 30 minutes.
- Tips: If you forget to take them out ahead of time, you can place them in a bowl of warm (not hot) water for about 10 to 15 minutes.

3 Milk and Cream:

- Time: About 30 minutes.
- Tips: Pour into a bowl and leave it out for a bit, or use warm water if you're in a hurry.

4 Yogurt or Sour Cream:

- Time: About 30 minutes.
- Tips: Just like with milk, leaving it out in a bowl will help it warm up.

5 Flour and Other Dry Ingredients:

- Time: Usually, they don't need to come to room temperature, but it's best to store them in a cool, dry place. If they've been in the fridge, a little time (10 to 15 minutes) at room temperature can help.

THE BAKER'S KIT

NEW BAKER'S BEGINNING KIT

To all my beginner bakers, I want you to remember to start from where you are with your baking experience. Don't rush ahead or get overwhelmed; just take it one step at a time and enjoy the process. Here's a basic list of items you need to get started on your baking journey:

1 **Large Mixing Bowl:**
- Essential for mixing batters, doughs, and combining ingredients. Look for a sturdy, non-slip bowl that can handle heavy mixtures.

2 **Handheld Mixer or Stand Mixer:**
- Handheld Mixer: Great for quick mixing tasks and easy to store.
- Stand Mixer: Ideal for larger batches and more intensive mixing. A stand mixer with a paddle attachment is perfect for pound cakes and other thick batters.

3 **Measuring Cups and Measuring Spoons:**
- Accurate measurements are crucial in baking. A set of dry measuring cups (for solids) and liquid measuring cups (with pour spouts) is essential, along with a set of measuring spoons.

4 **Spatulas:**
- Rubber Spatula: Perfect for scraping down the sides of bowls and folding in ingredients.
- Offset Spatula: Great for smoothing icing on cakes and lifting baked goods from pans.

5 10-Inch Baking Pans:

- Tube Pan or Bundt Pan: Perfect for making pound cakes, ensuring even baking and easy release.

6 10-Inch Round Cake Boards:

- Useful for transporting and displaying cakes. They provide stability for decorated cakes and make serving easier.

7 Sifter:

- A handheld sifter is useful for aerating flour and ensuring that dry ingredients are well combined, especially for delicate cakes.

8 Cooling Rack:

- Essential for cooling baked goods evenly after they come out of the oven, preventing sogginess on the bottom.

9 Oven Mitts or Pot Holders:

- Protect your hands while removing hot pans from the oven. Look for thick, heat-resistant mitts.

10 Baking Spray or Butter:

- A non-stick baking spray with flour can make greasing pans effortless, or you can use butter and flour as a traditional method.

11 Digital Kitchen Scale (Optional):

- For precision baking, especially with recipes that use weight measurements. A scale can help ensure accurate ingredient proportions.

12 Oven Thermometer:

- An essential tool for checking that your oven is at the correct temperature. Ovens can often be inaccurate, and having a thermometer helps ensure your baked goods are cooked properly.

13 Timer:

- A kitchen timer or the timer on your phone can help keep track of baking times to prevent overbaking.

14 Apron:

- A durable apron to protect your clothing while baking, ensuring you can work without worry about spills or messes.

15 Kitchen Towels:

- A set of clean kitchen towels for wiping surfaces, drying hands, and handling hot pans.

16 Recipe Book or Binder:

- Having a collection of beginner-friendly recipes can inspire new bakers. Consider including classic pound cake recipes and tips for baking success.

THE RECIPES

Alright, Cuties!

Now that we've covered all the fundamentals, are you ready to bake? If you're feeling excited to create something delicious, just stroll through the table of contents and find one of the 25 fabulous pound cakes you want to bake first!

Whether you're in the mood for a classic pound cake, a fruity twist, or a decadent chocolate delight, there's something for everyone. So, grab your apron, preheat that oven, and let's get baking!

Happy Baking!

SWEET POTATO POUND

SWEET POTATO POUND

Sweet Potato Pound Cake is the ultimate crowd-pleaser! Whether Thanksgiving, Christmas, or a cozy fall gathering, this classic dessert brings warmth, comfort, and that irresistible blend of sweetness and spice. The perfect dessert for holidays when you want to impress your guests and keep them coming back for seconds!

Dry Ingredients (Sift Together and Set Aside)

- 3 ½ cups all-purpose flour
- 2 teaspoons baking powder
- 1 teaspoon baking soda
- ½ teaspoon salt
- 2 teaspoons cinnamon
- ¼ teaspoon nutmeg

Wet Ingredients (Mix and Set Aside)

3 sticks unsalted butter (room temperature), 1 ½ cups granulated sugar, 1 cup firmly packed dark brown sugar, 4 eggs, 1 ½ cups baked and mashed sweet potatoes (room temperature), 1 tablespoon molasses, 2 teaspoons vanilla extract, 1 cup milk, 2 tablespoons sour cream

1 Instructions
Preheat the Oven to 340°F (170°C). Prepare a 12—to 16-cup bundt or tube pan by generously spraying it with baking spray with flour or greasing it with butter and flour. Set it aside.

2 Cream the Butter
Cream the butter in a large bowl for about 30 seconds.

3 Add Granulated Sugar
Add 1 cup of granulated sugar to the butter, and blend well. Then add the remaining ½ cup of granulated sugar and blend until well combined.

4 Add Dark Brown Sugar

Gradually add the dark brown sugar, blending until the mixture is light and fluffy (about 5-7 minutes). Remember to scrape down the sides of your bowl.

5 Incorporate Eggs

Add eggs one at a time, mixing well after each addition until yolk disappears

6 Add Sweet Potato, Vanilla, and Molasses

Add the room-temperature mashed sweet potatoes, vanilla extract, and molasses, and blend until smooth and well combined.

7 Alternate Adding Dry and Wet Ingredients

Gradually add the sifted flour mixture to the batter, alternating with the milk mixture. Begin and end with the flour mixture, ensuring to mix just until combined after each addition. Scrape down the sides of your bowl as needed.

8 Bake

Pour the batter into the prepared bundt or tube pan. Bake for 1 hour and 10 minutes, or until a toothpick or butter knife inserted in the center comes out clean.

9 Cool

Allow the cake to cool in the pan on a cooling rack for 10 minutes before flipping the cake out of the pan to cool completely.

CREAM CHEESE CINNAMON GLAZE

- 3 tablespoons melted butter
- ¼ cup of milk
- 1 tablespoon dark brown sugar
- ½ teaspoon cinnamon
- 3 cups powdered sugar

In a microwave-safe bowl, combine the melted butter, milk, dark brown sugar, and cinnamon. Microwave for 20-30 seconds, just until warm.

Stir in the powdered sugar and mix until the glaze is creamy and smooth. If the glaze is too thin, add more powdered sugar; if too thick, add more milk to reach your desired consistency.

Drizzle the glaze over the cooled sweet potato pound cake and enjoy!

SWEET CLASSIC POUND

SWEET CLASSIC POUND

This timeless dessert shines at family reunions, summer picnics, and Sunday brunches. Its buttery richness pairs perfectly with fresh fruit, whipped cream, or just as it is! Whether you're celebrating a special occasion or simply gathering with loved ones, a classic pound cake is the go-to treat that never disappoints!"

Ingredients
- 4 sticks (2 cups) of salted butter, at room temperature
- 3¼ cups of cake flour
- 1 teaspoon of baking powder
- ½ teaspoon of salt
- 6 large eggs, at room temperature
- 3 cups of white sugar
- 1 cup of half & half
- 2 tablespoons of sour cream
- 1 teaspoon of vanilla extract
- ½ teaspoon of lemon extract

Instructions

1 Preheat Oven to 330°F (163°C). Grease and flour a 12-cup Bundt or tube pan, making sure every crevice is covered.

2 **Prepare Dry Ingredients:** In a medium bowl, whisk together the flour, baking powder, and salt. Sift them if you're using a mix of all-purpose and cake flour to ensure even texture.

3 **Cream the Butter and Sugar:** In a large mixing bowl, beat the softened butter for about 3 minutes, until light and fluffy. Gradually add the sugar and continue beating for an additional 7-8 minutes, until the mixture is pale and fluffy.

4 **Add the Eggs:** Add eggs one at a time, beating well after each addition but only until the yolk disappears (about 15 seconds per egg).

5 **Add Flavoring:** Stir in the vanilla and lemon extracts.

6 **Combine Wet and Dry Ingredients:** Gradually add the flour mixture to the butter mixture, alternating with the half & half and sour cream mixture. Beginning and ending with the dry ingredients. Mix until just combined, being careful not to overmix.

7 **Pour and Bake:** Pour the batter into the prepared pan and smooth the top. Bake for 1 hour and 5 minutes to 1 hour and 15 minutes, or until a toothpick inserted into the center comes out clean.

8 **Cool:** Let the cake cool in the pan for about 10 minutes before transferring it to a wire rack to cool completely.

DELUXE VANILLA GLAZE

For a rich, silky finish, this vanilla glaze adds a touch of elegance to the cake.

- 2 cups powdered sugar
- 2 tablespoons whole milk
- 1 tablespoon heavy whipping cream
- 1 teaspoon vanilla extract

In a bowl, whisk together the powdered sugar, milk, cream, and vanilla extract until smooth.

Drizzle over the cooled cake for a luxurious, glossy finish.

MOSCATO CREAM POUND

MOSCATO POUND

Perfect for bridal showers, birthdays, and sophisticated soirées, this dessert adds a touch of elegance with its light, fruity flavor and creamy texture. Whether you're toasting with friends or celebrating love and laughter, this grown-up twist on a classic will have everyone swooning for more!

Ingredients
- 3 sticks (1.5 cups) of salted butter, softened
- 2 1/2 cups granulated sugar
- 5 large eggs
- 3 1/4 cups all-purpose flour (white lily or swans down)
- 1 teaspoon baking powder
- 1/2 teaspoon salt
- 1/2 cup Moscato wine
- 1/2 cup heavy cream
- 2 tablespoons of Sour Cream
- 2 teaspoons vanilla extract

Instructions

1 Preheat your oven to 330°F (163°C). Grease and flour a bundt cake pan or tube pan.

2 In a large mixing bowl, cream together the softened butter and sugar until light and fluffy.

3 Add the eggs one at a time, beating well after each addition.

4 In a separate bowl, whisk together the flour, baking powder, and salt.

5 Gradually add the dry ingredients to the butter mixture, alternating with the Moscato wine and heavy cream. Begin and end with the dry ingredients. Mix until just combined.

6 Stir in the vanilla extract.

7 Pour the batter into the prepared 10-inch bundt pan and smooth the top.

8 Bake in the preheated oven for 50-60 minutes or until a toothpick inserted into the center comes out clean.

9 Allow the cake to cool in the pan for 10 minutes. After 10 minutes, carefully invert the cake onto a wire rack to cool completely.

10 While the cake is cooling, prepare the Moscato cream glaze:
   - In a small saucepan over medium heat, combine Moscato wine and heavy cream. Heat until it just starts to simmer, then remove from heat.
   - In a bowl, sift the powdered sugar to remove any lumps.
   - Gradually whisk the warm Moscato and cream mixture into the powdered sugar until smooth and well combined.
   - Stir in the vanilla extract

11 Pour the Moscato cream glaze over the cooled cake, allowing it to drizzle down the sides.

12 Prepare the Berry Compote:
   - In a saucepan, combine mixed berries, granulated sugar, and lemon juice.
   - Cook over medium heat, stirring occasionally, until the berries break down and release their juices. Simmer for an additional 5-7 minutes until the compote thickens slightly.
   - Allow the compote to cool before spooning it over slices of the Moscato Cream Pound Cake.

13 Optional: Garnish with additional fresh berries or a dusting of powdered sugar.

14 Slice and enjoy your delicious Moscato Cream Pound Cake with a delightful wine-infused glaze and berry compote!

MOSCATO CREAM GLAZE

- 1/4 cup Moscato wine
- 1/4 cup heavy cream
- 1 cup powdered sugar
- 1 teaspoon vanilla extract

○ In a small saucepan over medium heat, combine Moscato wine and heavy cream. Heat until it just starts to simmer, then remove from heat.
○ In a bowl, sift the powdered sugar to remove any lumps.
○ Gradually whisk the warm Moscato and cream mixture into the powdered sugar until smooth and well combined.
○ Stir in the vanilla extract.

BERRY COMPOTE

- 2 cups mixed berries (strawberries, blueberries, raspberries)
- 1/4 cup granulated sugar
- 1 tablespoon lemon juice

○ In a saucepan, combine mixed berries, granulated sugar, and lemon juice.
○ Cook over medium heat, stirring occasionally, until the berries break down and release their juices. Simmer for an additional 5-7 minutes until the compote thickens slightly.
○ Allow the compote to cool before spooning it over slices of the Moscato Cream Pound Cake.

Dear Savory & Sweet Cuties & Princes,

While I'm excited to share delightful recipes that include alcohol as an ingredient, it is crucial to emphasize responsible and legal consumption. The use of alcohol in these recipes is intended for adults of legal drinking age only. It is important to be aware of and adhere to the legal drinking age in your respective region.

Alcohol can enhance the flavor profile of certain baked goods, bringing depth and complexity to the final product. However, it is essential to exercise caution and moderation when incorporating alcohol into recipes, as the cooking process does not entirely eliminate the alcohol content.

Please be mindful of your audience and ensure that your creations are enjoyed by responsible adults. Always store your baked goods in a secure manner to prevent unintended access by minors.

Let the joy of baking and the art of flavor exploration be a celebration of responsible and legal enjoyment.

Happy baking!

www.savoryandsweettreatsatl.com

EGGNOG POUND

EGGNOG POUND

This festive treat is a must-have for Christmas gatherings, holiday parties, and cozy winter nights by the fireplace. With its rich, creamy flavor and a hint of nutmeg, it's like the holidays in every bite. Serve it up with a cup of cocoa or coffee, and you've got the perfect dessert to spread the holiday cheer!

Ingredients

- 3 sticks of butter, softened
- 3 cups of sugar
- 5 large eggs
- 2 teaspoons of vanilla extract
- 3 1/4 cups of Swans Down Cake Flour
- 1 teaspoon of baking powder
- 1/2 teaspoon of salt
- Dash of nutmeg
- 1 cup of eggnog
- 1 tablespoon of sour cream

Instructions

1 Preheat your oven to 325°F (163°C). Prepare a 12-cup tube or bundt pan by greasing and flouring it or using a baking spray with flour.

2 In a large mixing bowl, cream together the softened butter and sugar for about 7 minutes until light and fluffy.

3 Add the eggs one at a time, beating well after each addition. Mix in the vanilla extract.

4 In another bowl, sift together the cake flour, baking powder, salt, and a dash of nutmeg.

5 Gradually add the sifted dry ingredients to the butter-sugar mixture in three parts, alternating with the egg nog mixed with sour cream. Begin and end with the flour mixture.

6 Once all ingredients are combined and the batter is smooth, pour it into the prepared pan.

7 Bake the cake in the preheated oven for approximately 1 hour to 1 hour and 10 minutes. Start checking for doneness at the 1-hour mark by inserting a toothpick into the center; if it comes out clean or with a few crumbs (not wet batter), the cake is done. Remove it from the oven and allow it to cool in the pan for about 15 minutes before transferring it to a wire rack to cool completely.

BACARDI GLAZE

- 3 tablespoons of Bacardi rum
- 2 1/2 cups of powdered sugar
- 1 tablespoon of milk
- 2 tablespoons of melted butter

In a mixing bowl, combine the Bacardi rum, powdered sugar, milk, and melted butter. Whisk together until the glaze is smooth and reaches a drizzling consistency.

Once the cake has cooled, place it on a serving plate and generously drizzle the Bacardi glaze over the top of the cake, allowing it to run down the sides.

Slice and serve the delicious Eggnog Pound Cake with the delightful Bacardi Glaze. Enjoy!

VANILLA LOAF POUND

VANILLA LOAF POUND

Whether it's a casual tea party, a simple Sunday afternoon, or even a last-minute gathering, this classic cake never fails to deliver. Its soft, buttery flavor pairs perfectly with your favorite toppings, from berries to ice cream.

Ingredients

- 2 cups all-purpose flour
- 1/2 teaspoon baking soda
- 1/4 teaspoon salt
- 1/2 cup salted butter, softened
- 1 cup granulated sugar
- 3 large eggs, at room temperature
- 1/2 cup sour cream or Greek yogurt
- 2 tablespoons of whole milk
- 2 teaspoons pure vanilla extract

1 Preheat your oven to 330°F (165°C). Grease and flour a 9x5-inch loaf pan or line it with parchment paper.

2 In a medium bowl, whisk together the flour, baking soda, and salt. Set it aside.

3 In a large mixing bowl, cream together the softened salted butter and sugar until light and fluffy (about 5 minutes) using a hand mixer or stand mixer fitted with a paddle attachment.

4 Add the eggs one at a time, beating well after each addition. Stir in the vanilla extract.

5 Gradually add the dry ingredients to the wet ingredients, alternating with the sour cream or Greek yogurt and milk. Begin and end with the dry ingredients, mixing until just combined. Avoid overmixing.

6 Pour the batter into the prepared loaf pan and spread it evenly.

7   Bake in the preheated oven for 50-60 minutes, or until a toothpick inserted into the center of the loaf comes out clean or with a few moist crumbs.

8   Remove the loaf from the oven and let it cool in the pan for 10 minutes before transferring it to a wire rack to cool completely.

9   Slice and enjoy your perfectly baked vanilla loaf!

STRAWBERRY SWIRL POUND

STRAWBERRY SWIRL POUND

Ingredients
- 3 sticks salted butter (room temperature)
- 3 1/4 cups all-purpose flour
- 3 cups sugar
- 1/2 cup homemade strawberry compote (recipe below)
- 2 teaspoons vanilla extract
- 6 large eggs
- 8oz sour cream
- 1/2 teaspoon baking soda
- 1/4 teaspoon salt
- 3 tablespoons strawberry gelatin
- - 1 teaspoon strawberry extract

Ideal for Easter brunches, garden parties, or even a fun picnic in the park, this dessert brings a burst of berry goodness with every slice. With its vibrant swirl of strawberries, it's as pretty as it is delicious—perfect for those sunny days and special moments with friends and family!

1 **Preheat Oven:** Preheat your oven to 330°F (165°C). Butter and flour a bundt or tube pan.

2 **Cream Butter and Sugar:** In a large bowl, cream together the butter and sugar until light and fluffy, about 7 to 10 minutes.

3 **Add Eggs:** Add the eggs one at a time, beating only until the yellow yolk disappears.

4 **Prepare Sour Cream Mixture:** Mix the vanilla extract into the sour cream until well combined. Set it aside.

5 **Combine Dry Ingredients:** In a separate bowl, sift together the flour, salt, and baking soda. Gradually add this dry mixture to the wet mixture, alternating with the sour cream mixture, mixing just until combined.

6 **Fold in Strawberry Flavor:** Gently fold in the strawberry gelatin, strawberry extract, and 1/2 cup of the cooled homemade strawberry compote into the batter, ensuring it's well combined without overmixing.

7 **Pour Batter:** Pour the batter into your prepared pan, smoothing the top with a spatula.

8 **Bake:** Bake in the preheated oven for about 65-70 minutes or until a toothpick inserted into the center comes out clean.

9 **Cooling:** Allow the cake to cool in the pan for 7 minutes before flipping onto a cake board or plate to cool completely.

STRAWBERRY COMPOTE

- 2 cups fresh or frozen strawberries (hulled and chopped)
- 1/4 cup sugar
- 1 tablespoon lemon juice

STRAWBERRY GLAZE

- 3 cups powdered sugar
- 1/4 cup milk
- 1 teaspoon strawberry extract
- 1/4 cup homemade strawberry compote

1. Make the Glaze: In a bowl, whisk together the powdered sugar, milk, strawberry extract, and 1/4 cup of the cooled homemade strawberry compote until smooth. Adjust the consistency with more milk or powdered sugar, depending on your desired thickness.

2. Glaze the Cake: Once the cake has fully cooled, drizzle the strawberry glaze over the top, letting it flow down the sides.

SOUR CREAM POUND

SOUR CREAM POUND

Whether it's a family gathering, a holiday dinner, or even a cozy night in, this rich and moist cake brings all the homestyle vibes. Its smooth texture and subtle tang make it a perfect match for every season—top it with fruit in the summer or drizzle with caramel in the fall. This cake is the secret ingredient to making any event extra special!

Ingredients
- 3 1/4 cups White Lily all-purpose flour or Cake Flour
- 1/2 teaspoon baking soda
- 1/2 teaspoon salt
- 3 sticks of salted, softened
- 3 cups sugar
- 2 teaspoons vanilla extract
- 1 teaspoon lemon extract
- 6 large eggs
- 10 oz sour cream

1. Preheat the oven to 335°F. Prepare your Bundt pan by spraying it with Pam's baking spray or greasing it with butter and flour.

2. In a large bowl, sift together the flour, baking soda, and salt. Set it aside.

3. Using an electric mixer, beat the softened butter and sugar together for 7 minutes on medium speed until light and fluffy.

4. Add the eggs one at a time, beating well after each addition until the yellow yolk disappears into the mixture. Mix on low speed.

5. Stir in the vanilla extract and lemon extract until well combined.

6. Gradually add the dry ingredients to the butter mixture, alternating with the sour cream. Always begin and end with the dry ingredients. Mix on low speed until just combined. Do not overmix.

7 Spoon the batter into the prepared Bundt pan, spreading it evenly.

8 Bake in the preheated oven for 60-70 minutes, or until the edges are golden brown, the top is slightly cracked, and a toothpick inserted into the center comes out clean.

9 Allow the cake to cool in the pan for about 7 minutes. Carefully run a knife around the edges of the pan to loosen the cake, then turn it out onto a tray or cooling rack to cool completely. Once cooled, slice, serve, and enjoy your delicious Sour Cream Pound Cake!

BUTTER VANILLA GLAZE

- 1/4 cup (1/2 stick) unsalted butter
- 1 1/2 cups powdered sugar
- 2-3 tablespoons milk or heavy cream
- 1 teaspoon vanilla extract
- Pinch of salt (optional, to balance sweetness)

Melt the Butter: In a small saucepan, melt the butter over low heat until fully liquefied.

Mix in Powdered Sugar: Remove from heat and gradually whisk in the powdered sugar until smooth.

Add Milk/Cream: Slowly add the milk or heavy cream, 1 tablespoon at a time, until you reach your desired glaze consistency. The glaze should be thick but still pourable.

Add Vanilla & Salt: Stir in the vanilla extract and, if desired, a pinch of salt to balance the sweetness.

Drizzle: Once smooth, drizzle the glaze over your cooled pound cake using a spoon or pour it from a spouted container.

Let Set: Allow the glaze to set for a few minutes before serving for a beautiful, buttery finish.

This rich butter-vanilla glaze adds a luxurious touch to your cake with its velvety texture and deep flavor!

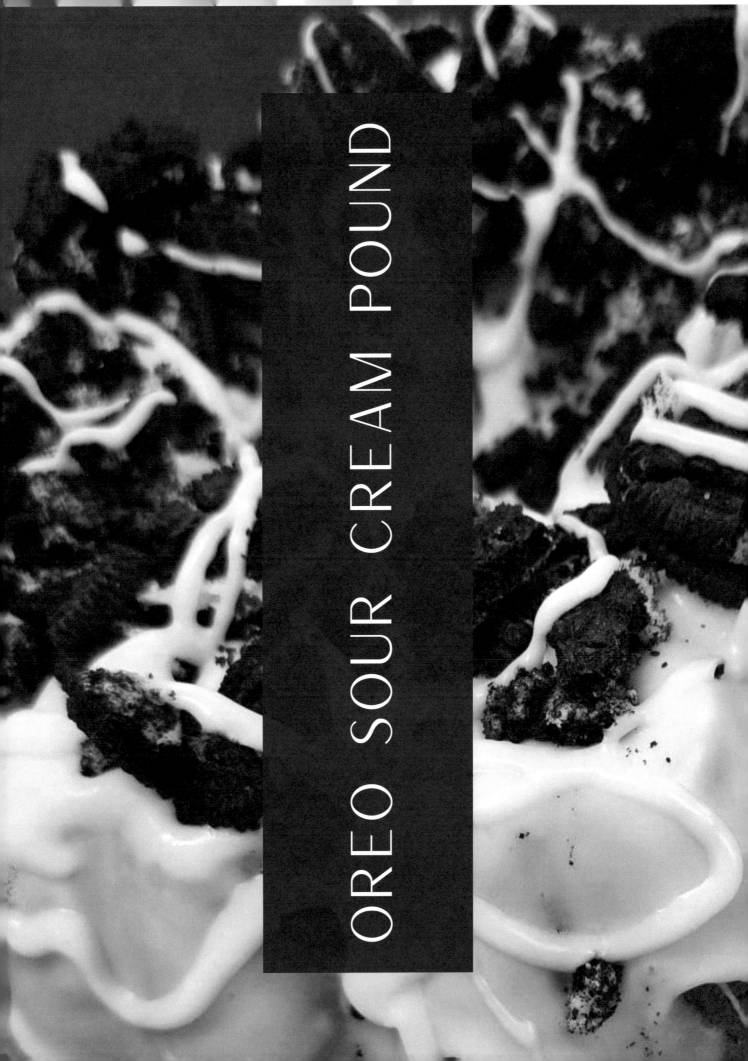

OREO SOUR CREAM POUND

OREO SOUR CREAM POUND

Enjoy your Oreo Sour Cream Pound Cake!
This rich cake combines the smooth texture of the pound cake with the crunch and creaminess of Oreo cookies, making it an irresistible treat!

Ingredients

- 3 1/4 cups White Lily all-purpose flour or All-Purpose Flour
- 1/2 teaspoon baking soda
- 1/2 teaspoon salt
- 3 sticks (1 1/2 cups) butter, softened
- 3 cups sugar
- 1 tablespoon vanilla extract
- 6 large eggs
- 10 oz sour cream
- 10 Oreo cookies, crushed (reserve a few crushed cookies for the top)

1 **Preheat Oven:** Preheat the oven to 335°F. Spray your Bundt pan with Pam's baking spray or butter and flour a 10-to-12-inch Bundt pan.

2 **Sift Dry Ingredients:** In a large bowl, sift together the flour, baking soda, and salt. Set aside.

3 **Cream Butter and Sugar:** Using an electric mixer, beat the softened butter and sugar together for about 7 minutes on medium speed until the mixture becomes light and fluffy.

4 **Add Eggs:** Add the eggs one at a time, mixing well after each addition. Be careful not to overmix, blending just until the yolks disappear.

5 **Add Vanilla Extract:** Stir in 1 tablespoon of vanilla extract.

6 **Alternate Dry Ingredients and Sour Cream:** Gradually add the sifted dry ingredients to the butter mixture, alternating with the sour cream. Begin and end with the dry ingredients, mixing on low speed until just combined.

58

7 **Fold in Oreos:** Gently fold in the 10 crushed Oreos, being careful not to overmix the batter.

8 **Transfer to Pan:** Spoon the batter into the prepared Bundt pan and sprinkle the reserved crushed Oreos on top for an extra crunch.

9 **Bake:** Bake the cake for 60-70 minutes, or until the edges are golden brown, the top is slightly cracked, and a toothpick inserted into the center comes out clean.

10 **Cool and Serve:** Let the cake cool in the pan for about 7 minutes. Run a knife around the edges, then turn the cake out onto a cooling rack.

OREO CREAM CHEESE GLAZE

- 4 oz (1/2 block) cream cheese, softened
- 1/4 cup unsalted butter, softened
- 1 1/2 cups powdered sugar
- 1 teaspoon vanilla extract
- 2-3 tablespoons milk or heavy cream
- 5 Oreo cookies, finely crushed (reserve a few for topping)

Cream the Butter and Cream Cheese: In a medium mixing bowl, beat the softened cream cheese and butter together until smooth and creamy.

Add Powdered Sugar: Gradually add the powdered sugar, mixing on low speed until fully combined and smooth.

Add Vanilla & Milk: Stir in the vanilla extract. Then, slowly add 2 tablespoons of milk or heavy cream. If you prefer a thinner glaze, add another tablespoon of milk until you reach your desired consistency.

Fold in Crushed Oreos: Gently fold in 3 crushed Oreos into the glaze mixture, leaving some small chunks for added texture.

Drizzle Over Cake: Once smooth, drizzle the glaze over your cooled Oreo Sour Cream Pound Cake.

Top with More Oreos: Sprinkle the remaining crushed Oreos over the top for a crunchy, eye-catching finish.

BISCOFF COOKIE BUTTER POUND

BISCOFF COOKIE BUTTER POUND

With its warm, spiced cookie flavor and rich buttery texture, this dessert is pure comfort on a plate. Perfect for when you want to impress your guests with something unique, this cake will have everyone asking for the recipe—guaranteed to be the star of the dessert table!

Ingredients
- 3 1/2 sticks (1 3/4 cups) salted butter, softened
- 2 1/2 cups sugar
- 6 large eggs
- 1/2 teaspoon salt
- 1 teaspoon baking powder
- 1/2 cup cookie butter
- 8 to 12 Biscoff cookies, crushed for added texture
- 1 1/4 cups heavy whipping cream
- 1 tablespoon sour cream
- 1 teaspoon vanilla extract
- 1 teaspoon of cookie butter flavoring or omit for another teaspoon of vanilla extract
- 3 1/4 cups cake flour or all-purpose flour

1 Preheat your oven to 330°F. Butter and flour or spray with baking spray in a bundt pan.

2 In a blender or stand mixer, beat softened butter for 1 minute. Gradually add 1 cup of sugar at a time, beating well after each addition until light and fluffy.

3 Add eggs one at a time, beating well after each addition. Then add cookie butter and extracts.

4 In a separate bowl, sift together the cake flour (or all-purpose flour), salt, and baking powder.

5 Add the sifted dry ingredients to the butter mixture gradually, alternating with the sour cream and whipping cream. Always begin and end with the flour.

6 Fold in the crushed Biscoff cookies gently.

7   Pour the batter into the prepared bundt pan and smooth the top.

8   Bake for 60 to 75 minutes or until a toothpick inserted into the center comes out clean. Allow the cake to cool in the pan for 15 minutes before transferring it to a wire rack to cool completely.

BISCOFF CREAM GLAZE

- 3 cups powdered sugar
- 3 tablespoons milk or heavy cream
- ½ cup of cookie butter
- 2 tablespoons melted butter
- 1 teaspoon vanilla extract

In a microwave-safe bowl, warm the milk or heavy cream, melted butter, and cookie butter for about 45 seconds. Mix until well combined.

Stir in the powdered sugar and vanilla extract until smooth.

Once the pound cake has cooled, drizzle the glaze over the top of the cake.

Optionally, top the glazed cake with additional crushed Biscoff cookies for extra crunch and flavor.

Allow the glaze to set before slicing and serving. Enjoy your delicious Biscoff Cookie Butter Pound Cake!

PECAN CARAMEL WHIPPING CREAM POUND

WHIPPING CREAM BUTTER POUND

Ingredients
- 3 1/2 sticks (1 3/4 cups) of salted butter, softened
- 3 cups of sugar
- 6 large eggs
- 2 teaspoons of vanilla extract
- 3 1/4 cups of cake flour or all-purpose flour
- 1/4 teaspoon of salt
- 1 teaspoon of baking powder
- 1 1/4 cups of heavy whipping cream
- 2 tablespoons of sour cream

Whether it's a baby shower, graduation, or a cozy family dinner, this velvety, melt-in-your-mouth cake is a crowd favorite. Its simple elegance makes it the perfect canvas for fresh berries, whipped cream, or even a scoop of ice cream. When you want to keep things classic but unforgettable, this cake is the way to go!

1 Preheat oven: Preheat your oven to 325°F (160°C). Grease and flour a 10-inch tube pan or bundt pan.

2 Cream butter and sugar: In a large mixing bowl, cream together the softened butter and sugar until light and fluffy. About 5-7 minutes.

3 Add eggs and extracts: Beat in the eggs, one at a time, mixing well after each addition. Stir in the vanilla extract.

4 Combine dry ingredients: In a separate bowl, sift together the cake flour (or all-purpose flour), salt, and baking powder.

5 Alternate adding dry ingredients and whipping cream: Gradually add the dry ingredients to the sour cream and heavy cream, alternating with the heavy whipping cream and sour cream. Start and end with the dry ingredients. Mix until just combined.

6 Pour batter into pan: Pour the batter into the prepared pan and spread it out evenly.

7 **Bake:** Bake in the preheated oven for 1 hour and 15 minutes to 1 hour and 30 minutes, or until a toothpick inserted into the center comes out clean.

8 **Cool:** Allow the cake to cool in the pan for about 15 minutes, then remove it from the pan and transfer it to a wire rack to cool completely.

9 **Serve:** Slice and serve the whipping cream pound cake on its own or with a dollop of whipped cream and fresh berries for an extra touch.

VANILLA BUTTER SIMPLE SYRUP

- 1/3 cup of sugar
- 1/3 cup of water
- 2 tablespoons of butter
- 1 teaspoon of vanilla extract

Combine sugar, water, and butter: In a small saucepan, combine the sugar, water, and butter.

Bring to a boil: Place the saucepan over medium heat and stir until the sugar is dissolved. Allow the mixture to come to a gentle boil.

Simmer: Reduce the heat to low and let the mixture simmer for about 5 minutes, stirring occasionally, until it slightly thickens.

Remove from heat: Once the syrup has thickened slightly, remove the saucepan from the heat.

Add vanilla extract: Stir in the vanilla extract. Adding the extract cools off the heat and helps to preserve its flavor.

Cool slightly: Allow the syrup to cool for a few minutes before using it.

Brush onto warm cake: While the cake is still warm, use a pastry brush to gently brush the vanilla butter syrup over the surface of the cake. Ensure even coverage.

Allow to absorb: Let the cake sit for a few minutes to allow the syrup to soak in and enhance the flavor and moisture of the cake.

Serve: Serve the cake slices with any remaining syrup drizzled over the top if desired.

PECAN CARAMEL SAUCE

- 1 stick (1/2 cup) of salted butter
- 2 cups of packed light brown sugar
- 2 cups of half and half
- 1/2 teaspoon of sea salt
- 1 teaspoon of vanilla extract
- 1 cup of chopped pecans

Combine butter, brown sugar, and heavy cream: In a large saucepan, melt the butter over medium heat. Add the packed light brown sugar and heavy whipping cream. Stir until the sugar is dissolved and the mixture is well combined.

Bring to a boil: Increase the heat to medium-high and bring the mixture to a boil, stirring constantly.

Boil for 8 minutes: Once boiling, reduce the heat to medium and let the mixture simmer for about 8 minutes, stirring occasionally. This will help thicken the caramel sauce.

Add sea salt and vanilla extract: After 8 minutes, remove the saucepan from the heat. Stir in the sea salt and vanilla extract. Mix until well incorporated.

Cool and thicken: Allow the caramel sauce to cool slightly in the saucepan. As it cools, it will thicken further.

Add chopped pecans: Once the caramel sauce has cooled and thickened to your desired consistency, stir in the chopped pecans until evenly distributed.

Pour over cake: Carefully pour the pecan caramel sauce over the top of your cake, spreading it out evenly with a spoon or spatula.

Serve: Serve the cake with pecan caramel sauce drizzled over each slice. Enjoy the delicious combination of rich caramel, crunchy pecans, and moist cake!

RED VELVET POUND

RED VELVET POUND

Whether it's Valentine's Day, an anniversary dinner, or a holiday party, this rich and velvety dessert adds a touch of elegance and indulgence to the moment. With its deep red color and a hint of cocoa, it's the perfect cake to make any gathering feel extra special and oh-so-sweet!

Ingredients
- 3 sticks (1 1/2 cups) of butter
- 2 tablespoons of canola oil
- 3 cups of sugar
- 2 teaspoons of vanilla extract
- 6 large eggs
- 1 and 1/4 cups of buttermilk
- 3 tablespoons of red food coloring
- 1 teaspoon of vinegar
- 3 cups and 1/4 cup of Swans Down (cake flour)
- 2 teaspoons of Hershey cocoa powder
- 1 tablespoons of sour cream
- 1/2 teaspoon of salt
- 1/2 teaspoon of baking soda

1 Preheat your oven to 330°F (165°C) and grease and flour a pound cake pan.

2 In a large mixing bowl, blend the butter and canola oil for 2 minutes until creamy.

3 Gradually add the sugar, one cup at a time, blending for about 7 minutes until light and fluffy.

4 Add the eggs one at a time, mixing well after each addition.

5 Stir in the vanilla extract.

6 In a separate bowl, mix the red food coloring into the buttermilk. Add the sour cream and vinegar to this mixture.

7 In another bowl, sift together the cake flour, cocoa powder, salt, and baking soda.

8 Begin adding the dry ingredients to the wet ingredients, alternating between the two, starting and ending with the dry ingredients. Mix until well incorporated.

9 Pour the batter into the prepared pound cake pan.

10 Bake in the preheated oven for 1 hour and 20 minutes, or until a toothpick inserted into the center comes out clean.

11 Allow the cake to cool in the pan for 10 minutes, then transfer it to a wire rack to cool completely.

CREAM CHEESE GLAZE

- 4 ounces of cream cheese, softened
- 1/4 cup of butter, softened
- 2 cups of powdered sugar
- 1 teaspoon of vanilla extract
- 2-3 tablespoons of milk (adjust to desired consistency)

In a mixing bowl, beat the cream cheese and butter until smooth.

Gradually add the powdered sugar and vanilla extract, mixing until creamy.

Add milk, one tablespoon at a time, until the glaze reaches your desired consistency.

Drizzle the glaze over the cooled pound cake.

Slice and serve. Enjoy your Red Velvet Pound Cake!

BAILEY'S CREAM CHEESE GLAZE

- 2 cups powdered sugar
- 2 oz cream cheese
- 3 tablespoons butter
- 2 tablespoons Bailey's Irish Cream
- 1 teaspoon vanilla extract
- 2 tablespoons milk
- 2 tablespoons heavy cream or coffee creamer

In a microwave-safe bowl, combine cream cheese, butter, Bailey's Irish Cream, vanilla extract, milk, and heavy cream (or coffee creamer).

Microwave the mixture for about 30 seconds until the ingredients are melted and well combined.

Remove the bowl from the microwave and gradually add the powdered sugar, stirring continuously until the glaze is smooth and creamy.

If the glaze is too thick, you can adjust the consistency by adding more milk or creamer, a teaspoon at a time, until the desired thickness is reached.

Once the glaze is ready, drizzle it over your favorite desserts such as cakes, cupcakes, or cookies.

Enjoy the delicious Bailey's Cream Cheese Glaze on your baked treats!

ALMOND HONEY POUND

ALMOND HONEY POUND

With its nutty almond flavor and a sweet drizzle of honey, this cake brings a touch of rustic charm to any occasion. It's light, flavorful, and perfect for sharing with friends and family when you want something elegant yet comforting!

Ingredients
- 3 sticks of salted butter, softened
- 3 cups of sugar
- 6 large eggs
- 3 cups + 1/4 cup of Gold Medal All-Purpose Flour
- 1 teaspoon of baking powder
- 1/2 teaspoon of salt
- 2 teaspoons of almond extract
- 1 teaspoon of vanilla extract
- 1 tablespoon of honey
- 1/2 cup of milk
- 1/2 cup of heavy cream
- 2 tablespoons of vanilla yogurt
- Sliced almonds (as desired)

1 Preheat your oven to 325°F (165°C). Grease and flour in a tube pan.

2 In a mixing bowl, beat the butter for 1 minute until creamy.

3 Gradually add the sugar and blend for 7 minutes until light and fluffy.

4 Beat in the eggs, one at a time, then mix in the almond extract, vanilla extract, and honey.

5 In a separate bowl, sift together the flour, baking powder, and salt.

6 In another bowl, mix the milk, heavy cream, and vanilla yogurt.

7 Gradually add the dry ingredients to the wet ingredients, alternating with the milk mixture. Begin and end with the dry ingredients.

8 Pour the batter into the prepared tube pan. Sprinkle sliced almonds on top and drizzle another tablespoon of honey over the batter.

9 Bake for 65-70 minutes, or until a toothpick inserted into the center comes out clean.

10 Let the cake cool in the pan for 7 minutes, then transfer it to a wire rack to cool completely.

SIMPLE SYRUP

- 1/2 cup of water
- 1/2 cup of sugar
- 3 tablespoons of butter
- 1 teaspoon of almond extract

In a saucepan, combine the water, sugar, butter, and almond extract.

Bring the mixture to a boil, stirring until the sugar is dissolved.

Remove from the heat and let cool slightly.

VANILLA ALMOND GLAZE

- 2 cups of powdered sugar
- 1-2 tablespoons of milk or heavy cream
- 1/2 teaspoon of vanilla extract
- 1/4 teaspoon of almond extract

In a small bowl, whisk together the powdered sugar, milk or cream, vanilla extract, and almond extract until smooth.

Drizzle the glaze over the cooled pound cake before serving.

Enjoy your homemade Almond Pound Cake with a delightful almond-infused syrup and a light vanilla almond glaze!

CHOCOLATE BUTTERMILK POUND

CHOCOLATE BUTTERMILK POUND

Perfect for birthdays, potlucks, or when you just want to spoil your guests with something decadent, this rich and moist cake is a total show-stealer. With its deep cocoa flavor and smooth texture, it's the kind of dessert that turns any occasion into a special event—one slice is never enough!

Ingredients
- 2 ½ cups all-purpose flour
- ⅓ cup unsweetened cocoa powder
- 1 ½ cups buttermilk, room temperature
- 4 large eggs, room temperature
- 2 ½ cups granulated sugar
- 3 sticks (1 ½ cups) unsalted butter, softened
- ½ cup semi-sweet chocolate, melted
- ⅓ cup sour cream
- 2 teaspoons vanilla extract
- 1 teaspoon baking soda
- 1 teaspoon salt

1 Preheat oven to 330°F (165°C). Grease and flour a 10-inch pound cake pan.

2 **Mix dry ingredients:** In a medium bowl, whisk together the flour, cocoa powder, baking soda, and salt. Set aside.

3 **Cream butter and sugar:** In a large bowl, beat the softened butter and sugar on medium speed until light and fluffy, about 3-4 minutes.

4 **Add eggs:** Add the eggs one at a time, beating well after each addition. Scrape down the sides of the bowl as needed.

5 **Mix in wet ingredients:** Add the melted semi-sweet chocolate, sour cream, and vanilla extract, and beat until combined.

6 **Alternate buttermilk and dry ingredients:** With the mixer on low speed, add the dry ingredients in three additions, alternating with the buttermilk, starting and ending with the dry ingredients. Mix until just combined, being careful not to overmix.

7 **Bake:** Pour the batter evenly into the prepared 10-inch pound cake pan. Bake for 60-70 minutes, or until a toothpick inserted into the center comes out clean or with a few moist crumbs.

8 **Cool:** Let the cake cool in the pan for 15 minutes, then remove it from the pan and transfer to a wire rack to cool completely before applying the ganache.

CHOCOLATE BUTTERMILK GANACHE

- 1 cup semi-sweet chocolate chips or chopped chocolate
- ½ cup heavy cream
- ¼ cup buttermilk
- 1 teaspoon vanilla extract
- Pinch of salt

Heat the cream: In a small saucepan, heat the heavy cream over medium heat until it begins to simmer (do not let it boil).

Melt chocolate: Pour the hot cream over the chocolate in a heatproof bowl. Let it sit for 2 minutes, then stir until the chocolate is completely melted and smooth.

Add buttermilk: Stir in the buttermilk, vanilla extract, and a pinch of salt. Continue stirring until the ganache is silky smooth.

Cool slightly: Allow the ganache to cool for 5-10 minutes, stirring occasionally, before pouring it over the cooled cake.

Assemble the cake: Pour the ganache over the cake, letting it drip down the sides. Let the ganache set before slicing and serving.

7-UP CREAM POUND

7-UP CREAM POUND

With its light, zesty flavor and refreshing hint of lemon-lime, this cake brings a burst of sunshine to any outdoor gathering. It's the perfect sweet treat to enjoy with friends and family, especially when you're soaking up those warm summer vibes. Trust us, one bite and everyone will be coming back for seconds!

Ingredients
- 3 ½ cups cake flour, sifted
- 1 cup 7-Up soda, room temperature
- 4 oz lemon yogurt, room temperature
- 3 sticks (1 ½ cups) unsalted butter, softened
- 5 large eggs, room temperature
- 1 teaspoon baking powder
- ¼ teaspoon baking soda
- ½ teaspoon salt
- 1 tablespoon lemon zest
- 2 teaspoons lemon extract
- 1 teaspoon vanilla extract
- 2 ¾ cups granulated sugar

1 Preheat oven to 325°F (165°C). Grease and flour a 10-inch pound cake pan.

2 **Mix dry ingredients:** In a medium bowl, sift together the cake flour, baking powder, baking soda, and salt. Set it aside.

3 **Cream butter and sugar:** In a large bowl, cream the softened butter and sugar together on medium speed until light and fluffy, about 3-5 minutes.

4 **Add eggs:** Beat in the eggs one at a time, mixing well after each addition.

5 **Mix in flavors:** Add the lemon zest, lemon extract, and vanilla extract, mixing until combined.

6 **Add wet ingredients:** Add the lemon yogurt and 7-Up soda, mixing until just combined.

7 **Alternate adding dry ingredients:** Gradually add the sifted dry ingredients into the batter, mixing on low speed until everything is incorporated. Be careful not to overmix.

8 **Bake:** Pour the batter evenly into the prepared 10-inch pound cake pan. Bake for 60-70 minutes, or until a toothpick inserted into the center comes out clean or with a few moist crumbs attached.

9 **Cool:** Let the cake cool in the pan for 12 minutes, then transfer it to a wire rack to cool completely before glazing.

LEMON-LIME GLAZE

- 2 cups powdered sugar, sifted
- 2 tablespoons fresh lemon juice
- 2 tablespoons fresh lime juice
- 1 tablespoon lemon zest
- 1 tablespoon lime zest
- 1-2 tablespoons 7-Up soda (optional, for thinning)

Combine juices: In a medium bowl, whisk together the lemon juice, lime juice, lemon zest, and lime zest.

Add powdered sugar: Gradually whisk in the powdered sugar until smooth and combined.

Adjust consistency: If the glaze is too thick, add 1-2 tablespoons of 7-Up to thin it out to your desired consistency.

Glaze the cake: Once the cake is completely cooled, drizzle the lemon-lime glaze over the top, letting it cascade down the sides. Allow the glaze to set before serving.

MARBLE POUND

MARBLE CREAM POUND

Ingredients
- 3 sticks of salted butter (room temperature)
- 3 cups of sugar
- 6 large eggs (room temperature)
- 3 cups plus 1/2 cup of Gold Medal All-Purpose Flour (sifted)
- 1/2 teaspoon of salt
- 1 cup of half & half
- 2 tablespoons of sour cream
- 2 teaspoons of vanilla extract
- 1/2 teaspoon of Creme Bouquet (optional)
- 1/2 cup of melted semi-sweet chocolate
- 1/4 cup of Hershey's cocoa powder

Whether it's a birthday, family get-together, or office party, this swirl of rich chocolate and vanilla makes it a dessert everyone will love. It's the perfect choice when you can't decide between flavors—why not have both? A timeless classic that brings a fun twist to any occasion!"

1 Preheat Oven
Preheat your oven to 330°F (165°C).

2
Grease a 10-inch bundt or tube pan with butter and flour or use a baking spray that contains flour.

3 Prepare Chocolate
Melt 1/2 cup of semi-sweet chocolate in the microwave in 20-second intervals, stirring after each interval until smooth. Set it aside to cool.

4 Cream Butter and Sugar
In a large mixing bowl, cream 3 sticks of salted butter for about 1 minute using a hand mixer or stand mixer on medium speed.

Gradually add the 3 cups of sugar, one cup at a time, blending for 1 minute after each addition.

After all the sugar has been added, continue to blend the mixture for an additional 7 minutes until light and fluffy.

5 Add Eggs and Extracts

Add the 6 large eggs one at a time, beating on low speed until each yolk is fully incorporated before adding the next.

After the last egg, blend for another 20 seconds to ensure the mixture is well combined.

Mix in the 2 teaspoons of vanilla extract and the optional 1/2 teaspoon of Creme Bouquet until well incorporated.

6 Prepare Dry Ingredients

In a separate bowl, sift together the 3 cups plus 1/4 cup of Gold Medal All-Purpose Flour and 1/2 teaspoon of salt. Set aside.

7 Prepare Wet Ingredients

Mix 1 cup of half & half with the 2 tablespoons of sour cream. Set aside.

8 Combine Ingredients

Begin adding the sifted dry ingredients to the butter mixture alternately with the half & half mixture. Start with a portion of the dry ingredients, mixing on low speed until just combined, then add a portion of the wet ingredients.

Continue alternating, beginning, and ending with the dry ingredients. Ensure each addition is well incorporated before adding the next.

9 Create the Marble Effect

Scoop half of the batter into the prepared bundt or tube pan.

With the remaining batter, gently fold in the 1/4 cup of Hershey's cocoa powder and the cooled melted chocolate. Be careful not to overmix.

Pour the chocolate batter on top of the plain batter in the pan. Use a knife or spatula to gently swirl the batters together, creating a marbled effect. Do not overmix to maintain distinct marbling.

10 Bake the Cake

Bake in the preheated oven for 60-70 minutes, or until a toothpick inserted into the center of the cake comes out clean.

Let the cake cool in the pan for about 15-20 minutes before transferring it to a wire rack to cool completely.

CHOCOLATE GLAZE

- 2 cups of powdered sugar
- 1/4 cup of milk
- 1/4 cup of cocoa powder
- 1 teaspoon of vanilla extract

In a bowl, mix 2 cups of powdered sugar, 1/4 cup of milk, 1/4 cup of cocoa powder, and 1 teaspoon of vanilla extract until smooth.

Once the cake is completely cooled, drizzle the glaze over the top.

LEMON SOUR CREAM POUND

LEMON SOUR CREAM POUND

Whether it's a birthday, family get-together, or office party, this swirl of rich chocolate and vanilla makes it a dessert everyone will love. It's the perfect choice when you can't decide between flavors—why not have both? A timeless classic that brings a fun twist to any occasion!"

Ingredients
- 3 sticks of salted butter (room temperature)
- 3 cups of sugar
- 6 large eggs (room temperature)
- Zest from 1 large lemon
- 2 teaspoons of lemon extract
- 1 teaspoon of vanilla extract
- 3 cups plus 1/4 cup of cake flour or White Lily all-purpose flour
- 1/2 teaspoon of baking soda
- 1/4 teaspoon of salt
- 10 oz of full-fat sour cream (equivalent to about 1 1/4 cups)

1 Preheat Oven
Preheat your oven to 330°F (165°C).

2
Grease a 10-inch bundt or tube pan with butter and flour or use a baking spray that contains flour.

3 Prepare Butter and Sugar Mixture
In a large mixing bowl, cream the 3 sticks of salted butter for about 1 minute using a hand mixer or stand mixer on medium speed.

Gradually add the 3 cups of sugar, one cup at a time, blending for 1 minute after each addition.

Continue to beat the mixture for an additional 5-6 minutes until it is light and fluffy.

4 Add Eggs and Flavorings

Add the 6 large eggs one at a time, beating on low speed until each yolk is fully incorporated before adding the next.

After the last egg, blend for another 20 seconds to ensure the mixture is well combined.

Mix in the zest from 1 large lemon, 2 teaspoons of lemon extract, and 1 teaspoon of vanilla extract. Blend until well incorporated.

5 Combine Dry Ingredients

In a separate bowl, sift together 3 cups plus 1/4 cup of cake flour (or White Lily all-purpose flour), 1/2 teaspoon of baking soda, and 1/4 teaspoon of salt. Set it aside.

6 Incorporate Dry Ingredients and Sour Cream

Begin adding the sifted dry ingredients to the butter mixture alternately with the 10 oz of full-fat sour cream. Start with a portion of the dry ingredients, mix on low speed until just combined, then add a portion of the sour cream.

Continue alternating, beginning, and ending with the dry ingredients. Ensure each addition is well incorporated before adding the next.

7 Prepare the Batter

Mix the batter until just combined and smooth, being careful not to overmix. Overmixing can result in a dense cake.

8 Bake the Cake

Pour the batter into the prepared bundt or tube pan, spreading it evenly.

Bake in the preheated oven for about 70-80 minutes, or until a toothpick inserted into the center of the cake comes out clean or with just a few crumbs.

9 Cool the Cake

Allow the cake to cool in the pan for about 15–20 minutes. Carefully invert the cake onto a wire rack to cool completely.

10 Serve

Once the cake is completely cooled, you can slice and serve it as is or dust it with powdered sugar for a simple finish.

LEMON GLAZE

- 2 cup of powdered sugar
- 2 tablespoons of milk
- 1 tablespoon of melted butter
- 2 tablespoons of fresh lemon juice
- 1 teaspoon of lemon zest (optional)

Mix the powdered sugar with the lemon juice, milk, melted butter, and zest until smooth.

Drizzle over the cooled cake for an extra burst of lemon flavor.

PINA COLADA CREAM POUND

PINA COLADA CREAM POUND

A tropical delight perfect for summer parties, poolside gatherings, or any event where you want to bring the island vibes! With its sweet coconut and pineapple flavors, this cake takes your taste buds on a mini vacation. It's the ultimate dessert for beach-themed parties, luau celebrations, or when you just want to add a little sunshine to your day!

Ingredients
- 3 sticks of salted butter (room temperature)
- 3 cups of sugar
- 6 large eggs (room temperature)
- 2 teaspoons of coconut extract
- 1 teaspoon of vanilla extract
- 3 cups plus 1/4 cup of cake flour (sifted)
- 1 teaspoon of baking powder
- 1/4 teaspoon of salt
- 1/2 cup of pineapple juice (from the can of crushed pineapples)
- 1/2 cup of heavy whipping cream
- 2 tablespoons of sour cream
- 2 cups of shredded coconut
- Small can of sweet pineapple juice

1 **Preheat Oven**
Preheat your oven to 325°F (163°C).

2 Grease a bundt or loaf pan with butter and flour or use a baking spray with flour.

3 **Cream Butter and Sugar**
In a large mixing bowl, cream 3 sticks of salted butter for 1 minute using a hand mixer or stand mixer on medium speed.

Gradually add 1 cup of sugar at a time, blending for 1 minute after each addition.

After the third cup of sugar, continue to blend the butter and sugar mixture for an additional 6 minutes until light and fluffy.

4 **Add Eggs**
Add the eggs one at a time, beating on low speed until each yolk is fully incorporated before adding the next. After the final egg, blend for another 20 seconds to ensure the mixture is well combined.

5 Prepare Dry Ingredients

In a separate bowl, sift together 3 cups of cake flour, 1 teaspoon of baking powder, and 1/4 teaspoon of salt. Set it aside.

6 Mix Pineapple Juice and Cream

Open a can of crushed pineapples and drain out 1/2 cup of pineapple juice.

Mix the pineapple juice with 1/2 cup of heavy whipping cream and 2 tablespoons of sour cream. Set it aside.

7 Combine Wet and Dry Ingredients

Begin adding the sifted dry ingredients to the creamed mixture alternately with the pineapple mixture. Start with a portion of the dry ingredients, mix on low speed until just combined, then add a portion of the pineapple mixture. Continue alternating, ending with the dry ingredients.

Gently fold in the shredded coconut by hand until evenly distributed.

8 Bake the Cake

Pour the batter into the prepared bundt or loaf pan, spreading it evenly.

Bake in the preheated oven for 60-75 minutes, or until a toothpick inserted into the center of the cake comes out clean.

Let the cake cool in the pan for 15 minutes before transferring it to a wire rack to cool completely.

9 Serve

Once cooled, you can serve the cake as is or add a glaze. A simple glaze can be made by mixing powdered sugar with a little pineapple juice or coconut milk.

COCONUT GLAZE

- 3 cups of powdered sugar
- 1/3 cup of pineapple juice
- 1 teaspoon of coconut extract
- 2 tablespoons of melted butter
- 2 tablespoons of milk

Mix the powdered sugar, coconut extract, melted butter, milk and pineapple juice or coconut milk until smooth.

Drizzle over the cooled cake before serving.

7-FLAVOR CREAM CHEESE POUND

7-FLAVOR CREAM CHEESE POUND

Ingredients
- 1 (8 oz) package Philadelphia cream cheese, softened
- 3 sticks (1 ½ cups) salted butter, softened
- 3 cups granulated sugar
- 6 large eggs
- 3 tablespoons of sour cream
- 3 cups + 2 tbsp White Lily all-purpose flour or cake flour
- ½ tsp baking powder
- ⅛ tsp salt
- 1 tsp vanilla extract
- ½ tsp almond extract
- ½ tsp lemon extract
- ½ tsp creme bouquet extract (Amazon)
- ½ tsp butter extract
- ½ tsp coconut extract
- ½ tsp cream cheese extract (Amazon)

With its rich, buttery texture and a delightful blend of seven flavors, this dessert shines at weddings, milestone birthdays, and holiday feasts. Each bite is a burst of creamy, flavorful goodness that keeps guests coming back for more. When you want to impress with a cake that's as bold as the occasion, this is the one!

1 Preheat Oven
Preheat the oven to 300°F. Grease and flour a 10-inch bundt or tube pan or use baking spray with flour.

2 Sift Dry Ingredients
In a medium bowl, sift together the flour, baking powder, and salt. Set aside.

3 Cream Butter, Cream Cheese, and Sugar
In a large bowl, cream together the softened butter, cream cheese, and sugar on medium speed for 5–7 minutes until light and fluffy.

4 Add Eggs
Add the eggs one at a time, beating well after each addition to ensure full incorporation.

5 Mix in Extracts
Add all the extracts (vanilla, almond, lemon, creme bouquet, butter, coconut, and cream cheese). Mix until well combined.

6 Combine Dry and Wet Ingredients

Gradually add the flour mixture to the butter mixture, and sour cream beating on low speed. Mix until just combined, being careful not to overmix.

7 Bake

Pour the batter into the prepared pan and smooth the top. Bake for 65–85 minutes or until a toothpick inserted in the center comes out clean.

8 Cool

Let the cake cool in the pan for 7–10 minutes, then flip onto a wire rack to cool completely.

7-FLAVOR SYRUP

- ½ cup sugar
- ¼ cup water
- 3 tbsp butter
- ¼ tsp vanilla extract
- ¼ tsp almond extract
- ¼ tsp lemon extract
- ¼ tsp creme bouquet extract
- ¼ tsp butter extract
- ¼ tsp coconut extract
- ¼ tsp cream cheese extract

Make the Syrup: In a small saucepan, combine the sugar, water, and butter. Bring to a boil, then reduce heat and simmer for 3–5 minutes until the sugar dissolves and the syrup slightly thickens.

Add Extracts: Remove the syrup from the heat and stir in all the extracts. Let the syrup cool slightly.

Brush the Cake: While the cake is still warm, brush the syrup generously over the cake, allowing it to soak in.

CREAM CHEESE GLAZE

- 4 oz cream cheese, softened
- 2 tablespoons of melted butter
- 2 cups of cups powdered sugar
- 2–3 tbsp milk (or more for desired consistency)
- ½ tsp vanilla extract

Make the Glaze: In a medium bowl, beat the softened cream cheese, melted butter until smooth. Gradually add the powdered sugar, milk, and vanilla extract, mixing until you achieve a smooth, pourable consistency.

Glaze the Cake: Drizzle the cream cheese glaze over the cooled cake.

COCONUT RUM POUND

COCONUT RUM POUND

Ingredients

- 3 ¼ cups all-purpose or cake flour
- 3 sticks salted butter, softened
- 3 cups granulated sugar
- 6 large eggs
- 1 tsp baking powder
- ½ tsp salt
- ½ cup coconut rum
- ½ cup heavy cream (mixed with 2 tbsp sour cream)
- 2 tsp coconut extract
- 1 tsp vanilla extract
- ½ cup sweetened shredded coconut (for topping before baking)
- 1 ½ cups sweetened shredded coconut (for topping after glazing)

Perfect for summer cookouts, island-themed parties, or even a laid-back holiday gathering, this cake brings a taste of the tropics to any celebration. With its coconut richness and a splash of rum, it's the ideal dessert for those who love a sweet treat with a little island flair!

1 **Preheat Oven**
Preheat the oven to 325°F. Grease a 10-inch bundt or tube pan with butter and flour, or use a baking spray with flour.

2 **Sift Dry Ingredients**
In a medium bowl, sift together the flour, baking powder, and salt. Set aside.

3 **Cream Butter, Cream Cheese, and Sugar**
In a large bowl, cream the softened butter and sugar together on medium speed for 5–7 minutes, until light and fluffy.

4 **Add Eggs**
Add the eggs one at a time, ensuring each is fully incorporated before adding the next.

5 **Mix in Extracts**
Stir in the coconut extract, vanilla extract, and coconut rum.

6 Combine Dry and Wet Ingredients

Gradually add the flour mixture, alternating with the heavy cream and sour cream mixture. Start and end with the flour mixture, mixing until just combined.

7 Top with Coconut

Pour the batter into the prepared pan and sprinkle the top evenly with ½ cup of sweetened shredded coconut.

8 Bake

Bake for 60–75 minutes, or until a toothpick inserted into the center comes out clean.

9 Cool

Let the cake cool in the pan for 10 minutes before flipping it onto a cooling rack.

COCONUT RUM SYRUP

- ½ cup coconut rum
- ½ cup sugar
- ½ cup water
- 3 tbsp butter

In a small saucepan, combine the coconut rum, sugar, water, and butter.

Bring the mixture to a boil, then reduce the heat and simmer for 3–5 minutes, stirring occasionally, until the sugar dissolves and the syrup thickens slightly.

Remove from heat and let cool slightly.

Brush Cake: While the cake is still warm, brush the syrup generously over the cake, allowing it to soak in.

COCONUT GLAZE

- 2 cups powdered sugar
- ¼ cup coconut milk or regular milk
- 2 tablespoons of rum
- 1 tsp coconut extract
- 2 tbsp melted butter

In a medium bowl, whisk together the powdered sugar, coconut milk, rum, coconut extract, and melted butter until smooth. Adjust the consistency as needed by adding more coconut milk or powdered sugar.

Drizzle: Pour the glaze over the cooled cake.

LEMON BLUEBERRY POUND

LEMON BLUEBERRY POUND

Ingredients

- 3 ¼ cups all-purpose flour
- 3 sticks salted butter, softened
- 3 cups granulated sugar
- Zest of 2 lemons
- 6 large eggs
- 2 tsp lemon extract
- 1 tsp vanilla extract
- 1 cup heavy cream
- 1 ½ cups fresh blueberries (tossed in 1 tbsp flour to prevent sinking)
- 1 tsp baking powder
- ½ tsp salt

Whether it's a baby shower, Easter brunch, or a sunny garden party, this cake bursts with zesty lemon and juicy blueberries. It's the perfect dessert for light, breezy occasions where you want to serve something sweet, tangy, and full of seasonal flavor!

1 Preheat Oven
Preheat oven to 325°F. Grease a 10-inch bundt or loaf pan with butter and flour, or use a baking spray with flour.

2 Sift Dry Ingredients
In a medium bowl, sift together the flour, baking powder, and salt. Set aside.

3 Cream Butter, Cream Cheese, and Sugar
In a large bowl, beat the softened butter, sugar, and lemon zest on medium speed for 5–7 minutes, until light and fluffy.

4 Add Eggs
Add the eggs one at a time, beating well after each addition to ensure full incorporation.

5 Mix in Extracts
Stir in the lemon extract and vanilla extract.

6 Alternate Dry and Wet Ingredients

Gradually add the flour mixture, alternating with the heavy cream, beginning and ending with the flour. Mix until just combined.

7 Fold in Blueberries

Gently fold the floured blueberries into the batter, being careful not to overmix.

8 Bake

Pour the batter into the prepared pan and smooth the top. Bake for 60–75 minutes, or until a toothpick inserted into the center comes out clean.

9 Cool

Let the cake cool in the pan for 10 minutes before flipping it onto a cooling rack.

LEMON BLUEBERRY GLAZE

- 1 cup fresh blueberries
- 3 cups powdered sugar
- 2 tbsp fresh lemon juice (about 1 lemon)
- Zest of 1 lemon
- 2–3 tbsp milk (adjust for desired consistency)
- 1 tsp vanilla extract (optional)

Cook the Blueberries: In a small saucepan over medium heat, cook the fresh blueberries with 1–2 tablespoons of water until they burst and release their juices, about 5–7 minutes. Stir occasionally. Once the blueberries have broken down, mash them with a fork or use a strainer to extract the juice, discarding the skins if preferred. Set the juice aside to cool slightly.

Make the Glaze: In a medium bowl, whisk together the powdered sugar, fresh lemon juice, and lemon zest.

Add Blueberry Juice: Add the cooled blueberry juice to the glaze and mix until smooth. If the glaze is too thick, add milk 1 tablespoon at a time to reach your desired consistency.

Optional Vanilla: For extra flavor, stir in 1 teaspoon of vanilla extract.

Drizzle: Drizzle the glaze over your cooled pound cake.

COCONUT LIME POUND

COCONUT LIME POUND

The ultimate tropical twist for summer picnics, pool parties, and backyard BBQs! With its refreshing lime zest and sweet coconut flavor, this cake brings a bright, island-inspired vibe to any sunny celebration. Perfect for when you want to serve up something light, fun, and bursting with flavor that feels like a mini vacation with every bite!

Ingredients
- 3 ¼ cups all-purpose or cake flour
- 3 sticks salted butter, softened
- 3 cups granulated sugar
- Zest of 1 lime
- 6 large eggs
- 2 tsp coconut extract
- 1 ¼ cups half & half (mixed with 2 tbsp sour cream)
- Juice of 2 limes (about 2 tbsp)
- 1 tsp baking powder
- ½ tsp salt

1 Preheat Oven
Preheat oven to 325°F. Grease a 10-inch bundt or tube pan with butter and flour, or use a baking spray with flour.

2 Sift Dry Ingredients
In a medium bowl, sift together the flour, baking powder, and salt. Set aside.

3 Cream Butter, Cream Cheese, and Sugar
In a large bowl, beat the softened butter, sugar, and lemon zest on medium speed for 5–7 minutes, until light and fluffy.

4 Add Lime Zest and Eggs
Add the lime zest, then mix in the eggs one at a time, ensuring each egg is fully incorporated before adding the next.

5 Mix in Extracts
Mix in the coconut extract and the juice of 2 limes.

6 Alternate Dry and Wet Ingredients

Gradually add the flour mixture, alternating with the half & half and sour cream mixture. Begin and end with the flour mixture. Mix until just combined; do not overmix.

7 Bake

Pour the batter into the prepared pan, smoothing the top. Bake for 60–75 minutes, or until a toothpick inserted into the center comes out clean.

8 Cool

Let the cake cool in the pan for 10 minutes before flipping it onto a cooling rack.

COCONUT LIME GLAZE

- ½ cup coconut milk
- Coconut extract
- 3 cups powdered sugar
- Juice of ½ lime
- 3 tbsp melted butter

In a medium bowl, whisk together the coconut milk, coconut extract powdered sugar, lime juice, and melted butter until smooth. If the glaze is too thin, add more powdered sugar. If too thick, add a little more coconut milk.

Drizzle the glaze over the warm cake.

Final Touch: Top the cake with 1 ½ cups of sweetened shredded coconut and a bit of extra lime zest for garnish.

MOUNTAIN DEW CREAM POUND

MOUNTAIN DEW CREAM POUND

Ingredients
- 3 ¼ cups all-purpose or cake flour
- 3 sticks salted butter, softened
- 2 ¾ cups granulated sugar
- Zest of 1 lime and 1 lemon
- 6 large eggs
- 2 tsp lemon extract
- 1 tsp vanilla extract
- ½ tsp baking soda
- ¼ tsp salt
- 1 cup Mountain Dew soda
- ¼ cup sour cream

Perfect for game days, tailgates, and fun family gatherings! With its citrusy kick and vibrant flavor, this cake brings an unexpected twist to any party. It's the perfect treat when you're looking to surprise your guests with something sweet, tangy, and totally unique—just like the event itself!

1 Preheat Oven
Set oven to 325°F. Grease a 10-inch bundt or tube pan with butter and flour, or use a baking spray with flour.

2 Sift Dry Ingredients
In a medium bowl, sift together the flour, baking soda, and salt. Set aside.

3 Cream Butter and Sugar
In a large mixing bowl, beat butter, sugar, and citrus zest on medium speed for 7 minutes, or until light and fluffy.

4 Add Eggs
Add eggs one at a time, ensuring each yolk disappears before adding the next. Continue mixing until all are incorporated.

5 Mix in Extracts
Mix in lemon and vanilla extracts.

6 Alternate Dry and Wet Ingredients

Gradually add the flour mixture, alternating with Mountain Dew and sour cream, beginning and ending with the flour mixture. Mix until just combined.

7 Bake

Pour batter into the prepared pan and smooth the top. Bake for 60–70 minutes, or until a toothpick inserted into the center comes out clean.

8 Cool

Allow the cake to cool in the pan for 7 minutes. Then flip onto a cooling rack.

9 Glaze

While the cake cools, prepare the glaze.

CITRUS GLAZE

- 3 cups powdered sugar
- Juice of 1 lime and 1 lemon
- 1 tbsp milk

In a small bowl, whisk together the powdered sugar, lime and lemon juice, and milk until smooth.

Drizzle the glaze over the warm cake.

PECAN BOURBON POUND

PECAN BOURBON POUND

A treat made for fall festivals, Thanksgiving feasts, and holiday gatherings! With its warm bourbon flavor and crunchy pecans, this cake brings a cozy, comforting vibe to any celebration. Perfect for those moments when you want to wow your guests with a dessert that's both indulgent and unforgettable!

Ingredients
- 3 ¼ cups all-purpose flour
- 3 cups granulated sugar
- 5 large eggs
- ¼ cup heavy cream
- 2 tbsp sour cream
- ¾ cup Jack Daniel's Tennessee Honey Whiskey
- 1 tsp baking powder
- 1 tsp salt
- 2 tsp vanilla extract
- Dash of nutmeg
- 1 cup crushed pecans (for lining the pan)
- 3 sticks (1 ½ cups) salted butter, softened

1 Preheat Oven

Preheat your oven to 325°F. Grease a 10-inch bundt or tube pan, then sprinkle the crushed pecans evenly in the bottom and along the sides of the pan.

2 Sift Dry Ingredients

In a medium bowl, sift together the flour, baking powder, salt, and a dash of nutmeg. Set aside.

3 Cream Butter and Sugar

In a large mixing bowl, cream the softened butter and sugar together on medium speed for about 5–7 minutes until light and fluffy.

4 Add Eggs

Add the eggs one at a time, beating well after each addition until fully incorporated.

5 Combine Wet Ingredients

In a separate bowl, combine the heavy cream, sour cream, and Jack Daniel's Tennessee Honey Whiskey. Set aside.

6 Alternate Dry and Wet Ingredients

- Gradually add ⅓ of the sifted flour mixture into the butter mixture and beat on low speed.
- Then, add ½ of the wet ingredient mixture (cream, sour cream, whiskey) and blend until just combined.
- Repeat with another ⅓ of the flour mixture, followed by the remaining wet mixture, and finish with the final ⅓ of the dry ingredients.
- Make sure to always end with the dry ingredients, and mix just until everything is incorporated. Be careful not to overmix.

7 Bake

Pour the batter into the prepared pan lined with crushed pecans. Smooth the top and bake for 65–75 minutes, or until a toothpick inserted into the center comes out clean.

8 Cool

Let the cake cool in the pan for about 10 minutes, then flip onto a wire rack to cool completely.

WHISKEY SIMPLE SYRUP

- ½ cup Jack Daniel's Tennessee Honey Whiskey
- ½ cup granulated sugar
- ¼ cup water
- 2 tbsp unsalted butter

Make the Syrup: In a small saucepan over medium heat, combine the whiskey, sugar, water, and butter. Stir until the sugar is completely dissolved and the mixture is smooth.

Simmer: Allow the syrup to simmer for 3–5 minutes until slightly thickened. Remove from heat and let it cool slightly.

Brush the Cake: While the cake is still warm, generously brush the whiskey simple syrup over the top and sides of the cake, allowing it to soak in. Apply multiple layers for extra flavor if desired.

KEY LIME POUND

KEY LIME POUND

Perfect for beach parties, tropical-themed events, or even a backyard BBQ, this cake brings a burst of citrusy goodness to every slice. Its tangy key lime flavor is the ultimate crowd-pleaser when you want to add a little sunshine to your dessert table and keep the good vibes going!

Ingredients
- 3 sticks (1 1/2 cups) salted butter, softened
- 3 cups granulated sugar
- 6 large eggs, room temperature
- 3 1/4 cups all-purpose or cake flour (sifted)
- 1/2 teaspoon baking soda
- 1/2 teaspoon salt
- 1 1/4 cups heavy cream
- 2 teaspoons key lime juice
- 1 teaspoon lemon extract
- 1/2 teaspoon vanilla extract
- 2 tablespoons lime-flavored gelatin (such as lime Jell-O)
- Zest from 2 whole limes

1 Preheat Oven
Preheat your oven to 325°F (165°C). Grease and flour a 10-inch pound cake pan or bundt pan.

2 Sift Dry Ingredients
In a medium bowl, sift together the flour, baking soda, and salt. Set aside.

3 Cream Butter and Sugar
In a large mixing bowl, using an electric mixer, cream together the butter and sugar for about 5-7 minutes, or until light and fluffy.

4 Add Eggs
Add the eggs, one at a time, beating well after each addition, until fully incorporated.

5 Add Flavors
Stir in the key lime juice, lemon extract, vanilla extract, lime gelatin, and lime zest. Mix well to combine.

6 Alternate Dry and Wet Ingredients

Gradually add the sifted flour mixture to the butter and sugar mixture in 3 parts, alternating with the heavy cream (starting and ending with the flour mixture). Make sure to mix just until combined after each addition, avoiding over-mixing.

7 Pour the Batter into the Pan

Pour the batter evenly into the prepared pound cake pan. Smooth the top of the batter with a spatula.

8 Bake

Bake in the preheated oven for 65 to 75 minutes, or until a toothpick inserted into the center of the cake comes out clean.

9 Cool

Let the cake cool in the pan for 10 minutes, then carefully invert it onto a wire rack to cool completely.

KEY LIME GLAZE

- 1 1/2 cups powdered sugar
- 2-3 tablespoons key lime juice
- 1 teaspoon lime zest

In a small bowl, whisk together the powdered sugar, key lime juice, and lime zest until smooth.

If the glaze is too thick, add more lime juice; if it's too thin, add more powdered sugar.

Drizzle the glaze over the cooled cake.

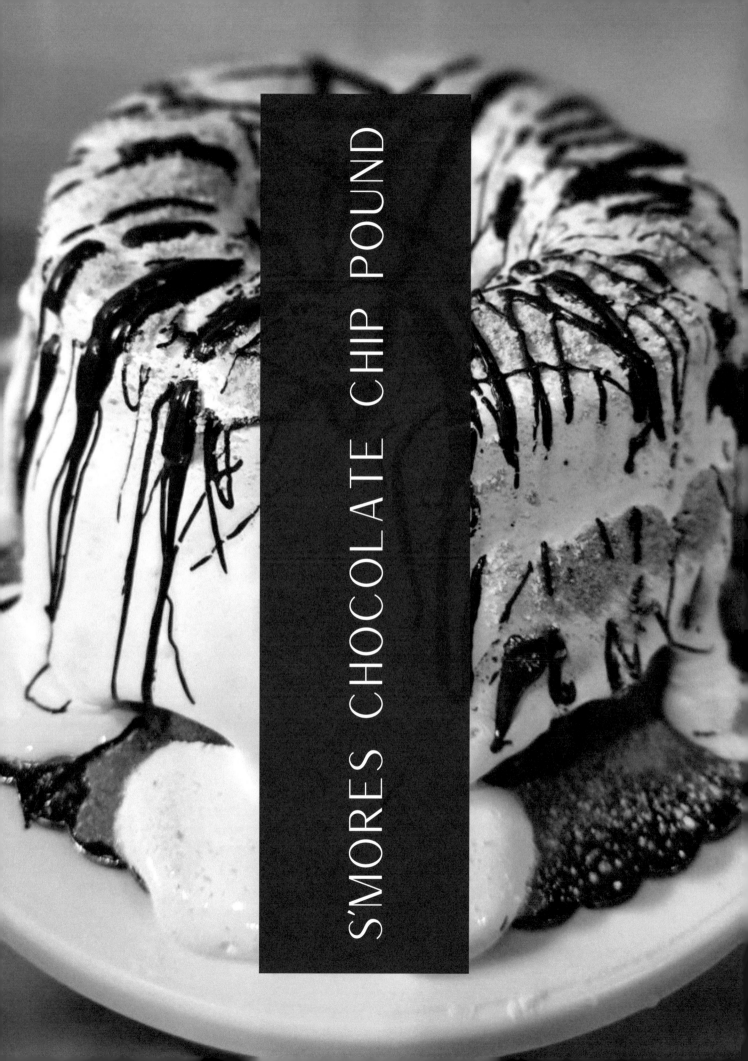

S'MORES CHOCOLATE CHIP POUND

S'MORES POUND

The campfire classic turned into a dessert masterpiece—perfect for cozy fall nights, camping trips, or family bonfires! With gooey marshmallow, rich chocolate, and graham cracker goodness baked right in, this cake brings all the nostalgia of s'mores without the mess. It's the sweet treat everyone will love when you want to make any outdoor (or indoor) gathering extra special!

Ingredients
- 3 cups granulated sugar
- 6 large eggs
- 2 tsp vanilla extract
- 3 ¼ cups all-purpose flour (or cake flour)
- ½ tsp salt
- ½ tsp baking soda
- 10 oz sour cream
- 1 cup chocolate chips (semi-sweet or milk chocolate)
- 3 sticks (1 ½ cups) salted butter, softened

1 Preheat Oven
Preheat your oven to 325°F. Grease and flour a 10-inch bundt or tube pan.

2 Sift Dry Ingredients
In a medium bowl, sift together the flour, baking soda, and salt. Set aside.

3 Cream Butter and Sugar
In a large mixing bowl, cream the softened butter and sugar together on medium speed for 5–7 minutes until light and fluffy.

4 Add Eggs
Add the eggs one at a time, beating well after each addition.

5 Add Vanilla Extract
Once the eggs are fully incorporated, mix in the vanilla extract until just combined.

6 Alternate Dry Ingredients and Sour Cream

- Gradually add ⅓ of the sifted dry ingredients to the butter mixture, and mix on low speed until combined.
- Add ½ of the sour cream and mix until incorporated.
- Repeat this process by adding another ⅓ of the dry ingredients, followed by the remaining sour cream, and finish with the last ⅓ of the dry ingredients. Mix until just combined, being careful not to overmix.

7 Fold in Chocolate Chips

Gently fold in the chocolate chips until evenly distributed.

8 Bake

Pour the batter into the prepared pan and bake for 65–75 minutes, or until a toothpick inserted into the center comes out clean.

9 Cool

Let the cake cool in the pan for 10 minutes, then flip onto a wire rack to cool completely.

S'MORES TOPPING

- 1 jar (7 oz) Jet-Puffed Marshmallow Creme
- ½ cup crushed graham crackers
- 3 tbsp Hershey's chocolate syrup

Spread Marshmallow Creme: Once the cake has cooled, spread the jar of Jet-Puffed Marshmallow Creme over the top of the cake. You can use a spatula or spoon to spread it in a thick layer.

Add Crushed Graham Crackers: Sprinkle the crushed graham crackers evenly over the marshmallow topping.

Drizzle Chocolate Syrup: Drizzle the Hershey's chocolate syrup generously over the marshmallow and graham cracker layer to complete the s'mores effect.

BROWN BUTTER VANILLA BEAN POUND

BROWN BUTTER VANILLA BEAN POUND

Perfect for weddings, afternoon tea, or holiday gatherings, its rich, buttery flavor and specks of real vanilla bean make it a timeless treat. Whether served on its own or with a side of berries and cream, this cake brings a touch of understated luxury to every celebration!

Ingredients
- 3 sticks of salted butter, at room temperature
- 3 cups of granulated sugar
- 6 large eggs
- 2 teaspoons of vanilla bean extract
- 3 1/4 cups of all-purpose or cake flour, sifted
- 1/2 teaspoon of baking soda
- 1/2 teaspoon of salt
- 10 ounces of sour cream

1 Brown the Butter
- In a medium saucepan, melt the 4 sticks of butter over medium heat.
- Continue cooking, stirring frequently, until the butter turns golden brown and develops a nutty aroma (about 5-7 minutes). Be careful not to let it burn.
- Once browned, remove from heat and let it cool slightly.

2 Prepare the Oven and Pan
- Preheat your oven to 325°F (165°C).
- Grease and flour a 10-inch bundt pan or loaf pan (you can also use baking spray with flour).

3 Combine Dry Ingredients
In a mixing bowl, whisk together the 3 ½ cups of flour, 1 teaspoon of baking powder, ½ teaspoon of salt, and a dash of nutmeg. Set aside.

4 Mix Wet Ingredients
- In a large mixing bowl, beat the browned butter (make sure it's not too hot) with 3 cups of sugar until well combined and creamy.

- Add the 6 eggs, one at a time, beating well after each addition.
- Mix in the 1 cup of milk, 2 teaspoons of vanilla bean extract, and 1 teaspoon of butter extract until fully incorporated.

5 Combine Dry and Wet Ingredients

Gradually add the dry ingredient mixture to the wet ingredients, alternating with the milk, starting and ending with the dry ingredients. Mix just until combined; do not overmix.

6 Bake

- Pour the batter into the prepared pan and smooth the top.
- Bake in the preheated oven for 60-75 minutes, or until a toothpick inserted in the center comes out clean.
- Let the cake cool in the pan for 10-15 minutes before inverting it onto a wire rack to cool completely.

7 Serve

Enjoy the cake plain or dust it with powdered sugar. This cake pairs beautifully with whipped cream or fresh fruit!

BROWN BUTTER GLAZE

- 1/2 stick (4 tablespoons) of salted butter
- 1/2 cup of milk
- 3 cups of powdered sugar
- 1 teaspoon of vanilla bean extract

- In a saucepan, melt the butter over medium heat. Stir continuously until it turns a golden brown with brown specks, being careful not to burn it.
- Remove the pan from heat and add the milk and vanilla extract.
- Gradually whisk in the powdered sugar until the glaze is smooth and flows easily. Adjust with a bit more milk if it's too thick.
- Drizzle the glaze over the cooled cake, allowing it to cascade over the edges.

BIRTHDAY CAKE POUND

BIRTHDAY POUND

Whether it's a milestone birthday or a simple get-together with friends, this rich, buttery cake is the perfect canvas for colorful sprinkles, sweet glazes, or fresh fruit. It's the go-to dessert that makes every birthday wish a little sweeter!

Ingredients
- 3 sticks (1 ½ cups) salted butter, softened
- 3 cups granulated sugar
- 6 large eggs
- 1 cup vanilla yogurt (plain or flavored)
- 2 teaspoons vanilla extract
- 3 ¼ cups cake flour (or White Lily flour)
- ½ teaspoon baking soda
- ½ teaspoon salt
- ½ cup sprinkles (plus more for topping)

1 Prepare the Oven and Pan
- Preheat your oven to 325°F (165°C).
- Grease and flour a 10-inch bundt pan or loaf pan (you can also use baking spray with flour).

2 Cream the Butter and Sugar
- In a large mixing bowl, cream together the 3 sticks of salted butter and 3 cups of sugar until light and fluffy (about 3-5 minutes).

3 Add the Eggs and Yogurt
- Add the 6 eggs, one at a time, mixing well after each addition.
- Mix in the 1 cup of vanilla yogurt and 2 teaspoons of vanilla extract until fully combined.

4 Combine Dry Ingredients
- In a separate bowl, whisk together the 3 ¼ cups of cake flour, ½ teaspoon of baking soda, and ½ teaspoon of salt.

5 Alternate Dry Ingredients and Sour Cream
- Gradually add the dry ingredient mixture to the wet mixture, alternating with the wet ingredients, and mix until just combined. Be careful not to overmix.
- Gently fold in the ½ cup of sprinkles until evenly distributed.

6 Bake
- Pour the batter into the prepared pan and smooth the top.
- Bake in the preheated oven for 65-70 minutes, or until a toothpick inserted in the center comes out clean.
- Let the cake cool in the pan for 10-15 minutes before inverting it onto a wire rack to cool completely.

7 Serve
Once cooled, you can top the cake with additional sprinkles or a simple glaze if desired. Enjoy your birthday cake!

VANILLA GLAZE

- 2 cups powdered sugar
- 3-4 tablespoons milk (or heavy cream)
- 1 teaspoon vanilla extract

Combine Ingredients
- In a mixing bowl, whisk together the powdered sugar and vanilla extract.
- Gradually add milk (start with 3 tablespoons) and whisk until smooth. If the glaze is too thick, add more milk, a tablespoon at a time, until you reach your desired consistency.

Drizzle on Cake:
- Once your Birthday Pound Cake has cooled, pour or drizzle the glaze over the top, allowing it to drip down the sides.
- If desired, sprinkle more sprinkles on top for added color and festivity.

Let Set:
Allow the glaze to set for a few minutes before slicing the cake.

ORANGE GRAND MARNIER POUND

ORANGE GRAND MARNIER POUND

With its bright orange flavor and a hint of Grand Marnier, this cake brings a sophisticated flair to the dessert table. Perfect for toasting to special moments and impressing your guests with a sweet, boozy twist!

Ingredients
- 3 sticks (1 ½ cups) salted butter, softened
- 3 cups granulated sugar
- 6 large eggs
- 3 ¼ cups all-purpose flour (or cake flour)
- ½ teaspoon baking soda
- ½ teaspoon salt
- 1 cup sour cream
- ½ cup Grand Marnier
- Zest of 1 orange
- 1 teaspoon vanilla extract
- ½ teaspoon almond extract (optional)

1 Prepare the Oven and Pan
- Preheat your oven to 325°F (165°C).
- Grease and flour a 10-inch bundt pan or loaf pan (you can also use baking spray with flour).

2 Cream the Butter and Sugar
In a large mixing bowl, cream together the 3 sticks of salted butter and 3 cups of sugar until light and fluffy (about 3-5 minutes).

3 Combine Wet Ingredients
In a separate bowl, combine the 1 cup of sour cream, ½ cup of Grand Marnier, and the zest of 1 orange.

4 Combine Dry Ingredients
In another bowl, whisk together the 3 ¼ cups of flour, ½ teaspoon of baking soda, and ½ teaspoon of salt.

5 Alternate Dry Ingredients and Sour Cream

Gradually add the dry ingredient mixture to the butter and sugar mixture, alternating with the sour cream mixture, and mix until just combined. Be careful not to overmix.

6 Bake

- Pour the batter into the prepared pan and smooth the top.
- Bake in the preheated oven for 65-70 minutes, or until a toothpick inserted in the center comes out clean.
- Let the cake cool in the pan for 10-15 minutes before inverting it onto a wire rack to cool completely.

GRAND MARNIER GLAZE

- 2 cups powdered sugar
- 3-4 tablespoons orange juice (or water)
- 2 tablespoons Grand Marnier
- Zest of 1 orange (for garnish, optional)

In a mixing bowl, whisk together the powdered sugar, orange juice, and Grand Marnier until smooth. Adjust the consistency with more juice or sugar as needed.

Drizzle the glaze over the cooled cake and garnish with orange zest if desired.

PEACH COBBLER POUND

PEACH COBBLER POUND

(Use The Classic Pound Cake Recipe on Page 36)

With its juicy peaches and golden, buttery crust, this dessert is a true crowd-pleaser. Serve it warm with a scoop of vanilla ice cream, and you've got the perfect treat to make any gathering feel like a home-cooked celebration of summer's best flavors!

Ingredients
- 1 can (29 oz) sliced Peaches, drained.
- 1 cup sugar
- 1/2 cup brown sugar
- 2 teaspoons vanilla extract
- 1/2 teaspoon lemon extract
- 1/2 teaspoon cake batter extract (optional)
- 2 tablespoons cornstarch
- 2 teaspoons Cinnamon
- 1/4 teaspoon nutmeg
- 1/2 stick melted butter + 2 tablespoons melted butter (reserved)
- 1 frozen pie crust (plus another half if desired for extra crust)

1 In a 9-inch round or square pan, combine drained sliced peaches, both sugars, vanilla extract, lemon extract, cake batter extract (if using), cornstarch, cinnamon, nutmeg, and 1/2 stick of melted butter. Mix thoroughly until well combined.

2 Break the frozen pie crust into pieces and place it on top of the peach mixture in the pan. Pour the reserved 2 tablespoons of melted butter over the pie crust.

3 Bake in a preheated oven at 425°F (218°C) for 30 to 40 minutes or until the peaches are tender, and the crust is golden brown. Allow it to cool while you prepare the pound cake.

4 Follow the instructions for **your chosen classic pound cake recipe**. Once baked and cooled, set it aside.

5 Once the peach cobbler is warm or cooled, spoon it generously over the pound cake, ensuring even coverage, including the center hole of the pound cake.

THE GLAZES

ORANGE CREAM GLAZE

- 3 cups powdered sugar
- ½ cup melted butter
- 3 tbsp fresh orange juice
- 1 tsp orange zest

- In a mixing bowl, whisk together the melted butter, orange juice, and orange zest.
- Gradually add the powdered sugar, whisking until smooth and creamy.
- Drizzle over your favorite cake and let it set.

LEMON GLAZE

- 3 cups powdered sugar
- ½ cup melted butter
- 3 tbsp fresh lemon juice
- 1 tsp lemon zest

- In a bowl, combine the melted butter, lemon juice, and lemon zest.
- Slowly mix in the powdered sugar until the glaze is smooth.
- Pour over the cooled cake and allow to set.

VANILLA-ALMOND GLAZE

- 3 cups powdered sugar
- ½ cup melted butter
- 2 tsp vanilla extract
- 1 tsp almond extract
- 2-3 tbsp milk (to thin, if necessary)

- Whisk together the melted butter, vanilla extract, almond extract, and powdered sugar.
- If the glaze is too thick, add milk a tablespoon at a time until you reach the desired consistency.
- Drizzle over your cake and let it set.

7 FLAVOR GLAZE

- 3 cups powdered sugar
- ½ cup melted butter
- 1 tsp vanilla extract
- 1 tsp almond extract
- 1 tsp lemon extract
- 1 tsp coconut extract
- 1 tsp butter extract
- 1 tsp cream cheese extract (optional)
- 2-3 tbsp milk (to thin, if necessary)

- In a bowl, combine melted butter with all the extracts and powdered sugar.
- Whisk until smooth. If needed, add milk for a thinner glaze.
- Drizzle generously over cakes for a flavor-packed topping.

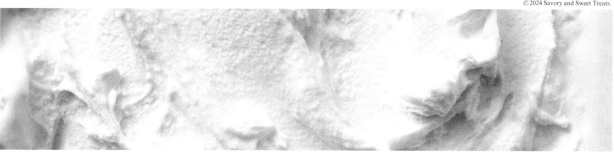

BUTTER GLAZE

- 3 cups powdered sugar
- ½ cup melted butter
- 1 tsp vanilla extract
- 2-3 tbsp milk (to thin, if necessary)

- Mix melted butter with vanilla extract in a bowl.
- Gradually stir in the powdered sugar until combined.
- Add milk to achieve the desired consistency and pour over the cake.

VANILLA BUTTER GLAZE

- 3 cups powdered sugar
- ½ cup melted butter
- 2 tsp vanilla extract
- 2-3 tbsp milk (to thin, if necessary)

- In a bowl, combine melted butter and vanilla extract.
- Gradually whisk in the powdered sugar until smooth.
- Add milk to thin if necessary, and drizzle over cake.

CHOCOLATE BUTTER GLAZE

- 3 cups powdered sugar
- ½ cup melted butter
- ½ cup unsweetened cocoa powder
- 1 tsp vanilla extract
- 2–3 tbsp milk (to thin, if necessary)

- Mix the melted butter, cocoa powder, and vanilla extract in a bowl.
- Gradually whisk in the powdered sugar until smooth.
- If needed, add milk until the glaze reaches the desired consistency. Drizzle over chocolate cakes or brownies.

MAPLE CINNAMON GLAZE

- 3 cups powdered sugar
- 3 tablespoons maple syrup
- 1 tablespoon melted butter
- ½ teaspoon cinnamon
- 2–3 tablespoons milk (as needed)

- Whisk together powdered sugar, maple syrup, melted butter, and cinnamon.
- Add milk a little at a time until the glaze reaches a pourable consistency.
- Adjust the thickness with more powdered sugar or milk as needed.

CHOCOLATE ESPRESSO GLAZE

- 3 cups powdered sugar
- 2 tablespoons cocoa powder
- 2 tablespoons brewed espresso or strong coffee
- 1 tablespoon melted butter

1-2 tablespoons milk (optional, for consistency)

- Combine powdered sugar, cocoa powder, and brewed espresso in a bowl.
- Add melted butter and whisk until smooth.
- Adjust thickness with milk or powdered sugar to get a smooth, shiny glaze.

COCONUT RUM GLAZE

- 3 cups powdered sugar
- 2 tablespoons coconut rum
- 1 tablespoon melted butter
- 2-3 tablespoons coconut milk (as needed)

- Mix together powdered sugar, coconut rum, and melted butter until combined.
- Add coconut milk gradually until you achieve a smooth, pourable glaze.
- Adjust consistency by adding more coconut milk or powdered sugar.

SALTED CARAMEL GLAZE

- 3 cups powdered sugar
- ¼ cup caramel sauce (store-bought or homemade)
- 1 tablespoon melted butter
- 1-2 tablespoons milk (as needed)
- Pinch of sea salt (optional)

- Combine powdered sugar, caramel sauce, and melted butter.
- Add milk as needed to thin out the glaze.
- Sprinkle a pinch of sea salt for a sweet-salty twist. Adjust with more powdered sugar or milk for the right consistency.

BROWN SUGAR BOURBON GLAZE

- 3 cups powdered sugar
- 2 tablespoons brown sugar
- 2 tablespoons bourbon
- 1 tablespoon melted butter
- 2-3 tablespoons milk or cream

- Mix together powdered sugar, brown sugar, bourbon, and melted butter.
- Add milk gradually to reach a smooth, pourable consistency.
- Stir until all ingredients are combined and the glaze is glossy. Adjust thickness as needed.

CREAM CHEESE GLAZE

- 4 oz cream cheese (softened)
- 3 cups powdered sugar
- 1 tablespoon melted butter
- 2-3 tablespoons milk or heavy cream (adjust for consistency)
- 1 teaspoon vanilla extract

- Beat the softened cream cheese in a mixing bowl until smooth and creamy.
- Gradually add the powdered sugar, mixing slowly to avoid clumps.
- Add the melted butter and vanilla extract to the cream cheese mixture, stirring until well incorporated.
- Slowly add milk or heavy cream, one tablespoon at a time, until the glaze reaches a pourable consistency. You can adjust the thickness by adding more powdered sugar if it's too thin or more milk if it's too thick.
- Whisk the glaze until smooth and creamy, ensuring it flows easily and can coat the back of a spoon.

LEMON CREAM CHEESE GLAZE

- 4 oz cream cheese (softened)
- 3 cups powdered sugar
- 1 tablespoon melted butter
- 2 tablespoons fresh lemon juice
- 1 tablespoon lemon zest
- 1-2 tablespoons milk (optional, for consistency)

- Beat cream cheese until smooth. Gradually add powdered sugar.
- Add melted butter, lemon juice, and lemon zest.
- Whisk in milk if needed to reach your desired consistency.

MAPLE CREAM CHEESE GLAZE

- 4 oz cream cheese (softened)
- 3 cups powdered sugar
- 1 tablespoon melted butter
- 3 tablespoons pure maple syrup
- 1-2 tablespoons milk (optional, for consistency)

- Combine cream cheese and powdered sugar.
- Add melted butter and maple syrup, mixing until smooth.
- Adjust with milk to thin if necessary.

CINNAMON CREAM CHEESE GLAZE

- 4 oz cream cheese (softened)
- 3 cups powdered sugar
- 1 tablespoon melted butter
- 1 teaspoon ground cinnamon
- 1-2 tablespoons milk or cream (as needed)
- 1 teaspoon vanilla extract

- Beat cream cheese and powdered sugar together until smooth.
- Add melted butter, cinnamon, and vanilla extract.
- Adjust thickness with milk or cream to reach the desired consistency.

STRAWBERRY CREAM CHEESE GLAZE

- 4 oz cream cheese (softened)
- 3 cups powdered sugar
- 1 tablespoon melted butter
- 2-3 tablespoons strawberry puree or strawberry syrup
- 1 teaspoon vanilla extract
- 1-2 tablespoons milk (optional)

- Beat cream cheese until smooth. Gradually mix in powdered sugar.
- Add melted butter, strawberry puree, and vanilla extract.
- Thin with milk if needed for consistency.

CHOCOLATE CREAM CHEESE GLAZE

- 4 oz cream cheese (softened)
- 3 cups powdered sugar
- 2 tablespoons cocoa powder
- 1 tablespoon melted butter
- 1-2 tablespoons milk or cream
- 1 teaspoon vanilla extract

- Combine cream cheese, powdered sugar, and cocoa powder.
- Add melted butter and vanilla extract, whisking until smooth.
- Adjust with milk for desired consistency, adding little by little.

CINNADOODLE POUND

CINNADOODLE POUND

With its warm spices and that irresistible snickerdoodle flavor, this cake is a crowd-pleaser for anyone craving a nostalgic twist on a classic dessert. Ideal for sharing with loved ones, it's the treat that brings all the cozy vibes to your celebrations!

Ingredients
- 3 1/4 cups Swan's Down Cake Flour or Gold's Medal
- 1 teaspoon baking soda
- ½ teaspoon salt
- 1 ½ cups (3 sticks) unsalted butter, softened
- 2 ½ cups granulated sugar
- 6 large eggs, room temperature
- 1 tablespoon vanilla extract
- 1 cup heavy cream, combined with ¼ cup whole milk

1 Preheat the oven to 325°F (165°C). Grease and flour a 10-inch pound cake pan.

2 Sift together the flour, baking soda, and salt in a medium bowl. Set aside.

3 Cream the butter and sugar in a large bowl until light and fluffy, about 4-5 minutes. Add the eggs one at a time, ensuring each is fully incorporated before adding the next.

4 Mix in the vanilla extract.

5 Alternate adding the dry ingredients and the heavy cream-milk mixture: Start by adding a third of the flour mixture to the butter mixture, followed by half of the cream-milk mixture. Repeat, finishing with the last of the dry ingredients, mixing until smooth.

6 Prepare the cinnamon-sugar filling by combining 2 tablespoons brown sugar, 2 tablespoons granulated sugar, and 1 teaspoon ground cinnamon in a small bowl.

7 Pour half of the batter into the prepared pound cake pan. Sprinkle 2 tablespoons of the cinnamon-sugar filling evenly over the batter.

8 Add the remaining batter and smooth the surface. Top with the rest of the cinnamon-sugar mixture, sprinkling it evenly over the batter.

9 Swirl the batter gently once with a butter knife to incorporate the cinnamon sugar into the batter.

10 Bake** for 65-85 minutes, or until a toothpick inserted into the center of the cake comes out clean.

11 Cool in the pan for 10 minutes before turning it out onto a wire rack to cool completely.

CINNAMON GLAZE

- 2 cups powdered sugar
- ¼ cup milk
- 1 tablespoon brown sugar
- ½ teaspoon ground cinnamon
- 2 tablespoons of melted butter

Mix powdered sugar, milk, brown sugar, and cinnamon until smooth and slightly thickened.

Drizzle the glaze generously over the cooled pound cake.

WHITE CHOCOLATE POUND

WHITE CHOCOLATE POUND

Ingredients
- 3 1/4 cups all-purpose flour or Swans Down
- 1 teaspoon baking powder
- ½ teaspoon salt
- 1 ½ cups (3 sticks) unsalted butter, softened
- 3 cups granulated sugar
- 6 large eggs, room temperature
- 2 teaspoon vanilla extract
- 1 cup white chocolate, melted and slightly cooled
- 1 cup heavy cream, combined with ¼ cup whole milk

With its smooth, creamy flavor and rich, velvety texture, this dessert brings a touch of luxury to the table. Whether it's Christmas, New Year's, or a cozy night with loved ones, this cake will have everyone savoring each delicious bite!

1 Preheat the oven to 325°F (165°C). Grease and flour a 10-inch pound cake pan.

2 Sift together the flour, baking powder, and salt in a medium bowl. Set aside.

3 Cream the butter and sugar in a large bowl until light and fluffy, about 4-5 minutes. Add the eggs one at a time, mixing well after each addition.

4 Mix in the vanilla extract and melted white chocolate until fully combined.

5 Alternate adding the dry ingredients and the heavy cream-milk mixture: Start by adding a third of the flour mixture, followed by half of the cream-milk mixture. Repeat, finishing with the last of the dry ingredients. Mix until the batter is smooth and creamy.

6 Pour the batter into the prepared pound cake pan and smooth the top.

7 Bake for 75-85 minutes, or until a toothpick inserted into the center comes out clean.

8 Cool the cake in the pan for 10-15 minutes before turning it out onto a wire rack to cool completely.

WHITE CHOCOLATE GLAZE

- ½ cup white chocolate, melted
- 2 tablespoons heavy cream
- 1/4 cup of milk
- 2 cups of powdered sugar
- 2 tablespoons of melted butter
- 1 teaspoon of vanilla extract

Melt the white chocolate and heavy cream together, stirring until smooth. Add powdered sugar, milk, extract, and melted butter and continue to stir or whisk.

Drizzle over the cooled pound cake.

PINEAPPLE UPSIDE DOWN POUND

PINEAPPLE UPSIDE DOWN POUND

Perfect for summer cookouts, family reunions, and tropical-themed parties, this cake combines juicy caramelized pineapple with a rich, buttery base that everyone loves. It's the ultimate crowd-pleaser for those who enjoy a sweet taste of nostalgia with a twist!

Ingredients

- 3 cups all-purpose flour (or White Lily)
- 2 teaspoons baking powder
- ½ teaspoon salt
- 1 ½ cups (3 sticks) salted butter, softened
- 2 ½ cups granulated sugar
- 5 large eggs, room temperature
- 1 teaspoon vanilla extract
- 1 teaspoon butter extract
- 1 cup heavy whipping cream
- ¼ cup pineapple juice
- ½ cup pineapple juice (reserved from the canned pineapples)

Topping Ingredients

¼ cup unsalted butter, melted | ½ cup packed brown sugar | 8–10 pineapple slices, canned or fresh | Maraschino cherries (optional)

1. Preheat the oven to 340°F (170°C). Grease a 10-inch round cake pan.

2. Prepare the topping:
   - Pour the melted butter into the bottom of the cake pan.
   - Sprinkle the brown sugar evenly over the butter.
   - Arrange the pineapple slices on top of the sugar, and optionally place maraschino cherries in the center of each pineapple slice. Set aside.

3. Make the cake batter:
   - In a medium bowl, sift together the flour, baking powder, and salt. Set aside.
   - In a large bowl, cream the butter and sugar until light and fluffy, about 4–5 minutes.
   - Add the eggs one at a time, beating well after each addition. Stir in the vanilla extract and butter extract.
   - Alternate adding the dry ingredients and the combined heavy whipping cream and pineapple juice to the batter: Start by adding a third of the flour mixture, followed by half of the cream-pineapple juice mixture. Repeat, finishing with the last of the dry ingredients. Mix until just combined.

4 Assemble the cake:
Carefully spoon the batter over the pineapple topping, spreading it evenly without disturbing the arrangement.

5 Bake:
Bake for 55-65 minutes, or until a toothpick inserted into the center comes out clean.

6 Finish and Serve:
- Once the cake is finished baking, remove it from the oven and let it cool in the pan for 10 minutes.
- Run a knife around the edges, then carefully invert the cake onto a serving platter.
- Pour the reserved pineapple juice** from the canned pineapples over the warm cake, allowing it to soak in for added moisture.

7 Cool and enjoy:
Let the cake cool slightly before serving. Serve with whipped cream or a scoop of vanilla ice cream if desired.

CALLING ALL
BAKERS &
ASPIRING BAKERS

Breakthrough
BAKING 101

Ready to take your pound cake to the next level? Join us for an interactive and fun course on baking a pound cake masterpiece.

SIGN UP

www.savoryandsweettreatsatl.com

THANK YOU

@savoryandsweettreatsatl | www.savoryandsweettreatsatl.com

- Lakeisha

Made in the USA
Columbia, SC
13 December 2024

6243c978-524c-4479-bb43-79467903c5f8R02